THE LAZY ENTREPRENEUR
37 HALF-BAKED MILLION DOLLAR IDEAS

Jeff Day

The information contained in this book is strictly for entertainment purposes. If you wish to apply ideas contained in this book, you are taking full responsibility for your actions, and there are no warranties, express or implied, that you will make even $1.00 from these ideas, much less $1,000,000. Sorry, my lawyers made me say it.

First paperback edition October 2018

Cover design by Joanie Cahill
Illustrations by Erin Leeder

ISBN 978-1-7328835-0-5 (paperback)

Published by: Fifth Times the Charm

One day I'm going to _____

HOUSE RULES: WHAT YOU NEED TO KNOW

1)   This book began as a passion project and is meant to be fun and entertaining. Please enjoy it that way. Like beers, it is best shared with friends.

2)   It's called The Lazy Entrepreneur for a reason. Might there be a few typos? Sure, there might be. I'm giving away millions, perhaps billions, of dollars. The least you can do is allow me to get away with a few grammatical errors.

3)   I don't claim to have invented or own the rights to any of these ideas. Want to start one of the businesses? Knock yourself out. Just remember me if you get rich. Seriously.

4)   In case it wasn't obvious, the Success Rating is nothing more than an arbitrary and completely subjective score intended to make this book appear more legitimate than it actually is. In other words, please don't go cashing in your 401k based on it.

5)   There's no right way to read this book. Front to back. Back to front. Or on shuffle. The choice is yours.

6)   Do you have a half-baked million-dollar idea and want to be a contributor to Volume II? Shoot me a note at halfbakedmilliondollarideas@ gmail.com and let's chat!

The Half-Baked Ideas

WATER WIGS

Contributors: Jeff Day & Mike H.

WHAT IS IT?

Every day millions of children flock to pools to cool off, play with friends, and enjoy games of sharks and minnows or Marco Polo. Kids are required to follow some basic rules: don't run in the pool area; don't dive in the shallow end; and don't pee in the water. But that's about it... in America. In China (and other Asian countries), there's a different kind of rule, one that presents an interesting business opportunity: swimmers are required to wear swim caps to get in the pool. Yes, that's right – those horribly ugly, outdated, and uncomfortable pieces of head-gear. In America, we're accustomed to seeing them worn by competitive swimmers, but rarely for recreational use. So, how can you capitalize on a global opportunity to make swim caps more appealing to children?

Introducing Water Wigs, swim caps for kids that have fun and imaginative attachments. You may have noticed that in recent years, the bike helmet industry in the US has been overtaken by the very same trend. In fact, that's the inspiration behind Water Wigs. Kids are required to wear helmets (either by law or their parents) and companies found a way to profit by making them more fun to wear. Water Wigs uses the same insight and applies it to the Asian swim cap market.

Water Wigs are swim caps with interchangeable attachments, so kids can constantly sport a new look. The cap itself is a one-time purchase, but kids (i.e. their parents) can purchase an endless array of cool attachments. Whether it be Mickey Mouse ears, a rainbow mohawk, or Jamaican dreadlocks, there's sure to be a Water Wig that makes pool time a whole lot more fun. Plus, once the "cool kids" start wearing them, the social pressure to fit in will spread like wildfire.

WHY IS IT NEEDED?

Water Wigs converts a required piece of swim gear from awful to awesome. Kids will be excited to show off their caps at the pool. Children love to express themselves and Water Wigs allows them another opportunity to do just that.

HOW DOES IT MAKE MONEY?

First and foremost, the Asian market is huge (1.4 Billion people live in China). Since essentially all kids want to go swimming, that means the market size for swim caps is pretty darn big. It doesn't take much market share to generate a million-dollar business in Asia. Specifically, Water Wigs works like the razor blade model: break-even on the swim cap and make all your money on the attachments. Once momentum builds, hold on to your trunks because a tsunami of sales is coming (this business lends itself too well to puns).

WHAT'S THE CATCH?

Ever tried launching a business in China? I didn't think so. There are a host of barriers to conducting business overseas, particularly in Asia. Not that I know or understand any of them, but I can only assume that's the case. So, while the consumer demand may exist, you may find yourself a fish *out* of water (yep, did it again).

WHAT'S THE LIKELIHOOD OF SUCCESS?

Success Rating: 50%

Forget million, Water Wigs could be a billion-dollar business. Kids will want them, and parents will feel good about buying them. However, there are far too many unknowns about operating in the Chinese market to give this anything more than a fifty-fifty chance of success.

THE WEDDING TREE

Contributor: Greg LeMay

WHAT IS IT?

Imagine for a moment that there was no tradition around opening gifts on Christmas morning. You still received your presents, but instead of seeing that beautiful mountain of wrapped goodies under the tree and opening them all at once, you received a slow drip of shipping boxes once Halloween passed and opened them whenever the mailman happened to drop them off. You'd end up with the same gifts as before, but it would take some of the magic out of it, right? Who doesn't like seeing that pile of Christmas gifts under the tree and anticipating what might be inside them? Like we all know, when you're forced to wait for something, it makes finally getting it feel that much better...

This no-fun Christmas I described is how most American couples do wedding gifts. There's no waiting period of anticipation. There's no watching the gifts pile up. There's no singular moment of revelry. Instead, boxes trickle in as guests visit the wedding website and it occurs to them to click over to the registry. Couples (if the first one home even bothers waiting for the other to get home) typically open the gifts as they arrive, perhaps to get a head start on the laborious task of writing thank you notes. But where's the fun in that? Simply put, there's never been a traditional way to celebrate the receipt and opening of wedding gifts... until now.

Introducing The Wedding Tree, a decorative tree that celebrates the engagement and impending nuptials of a loving couple. Like at Christmas, wedding gifts accumulate under the tree as the big day gets closer and closer. When the now-married couple returns to their new home, filled with youthful exuberance, they ceremoniously open their bounty. Easter has baskets. Lost teeth have pillows. Thanksgiving has turkey and drunk uncles. Matrimony now has a tree.

WHY IS IT NEEDED?

This is a wedding we're talking about, right? Like funerals and over-bearing pet owners, rationality be damned. There's no place for "need" when it comes to accepting (and paying for) wedding traditions. You know what else isn't *needed*? Embossed invitations. Menus with no options. Chargers. Or wearing something blue. But we do it because we're *supposed to*. Or because you're far too scared (and smart) to question your fiancée. Plus, we already know that 75% of couples have already done away with one traditional form of pre-marital anticipation, so there's definitely white space for some sort of build-up and release around the wedding day.

HOW DOES IT MAKE MONEY?

By getting The Wedding Tree into Emily Post's *Complete Book of Wedding Etiquette*. This turns what could at first blush be considered a gimmick into a bonafide wedding tradition. Will this be easy? No. Might it require giving kickbacks to every wedding planner in America? Quite possibly. But once you get enough traction, no couple will want to be without their own name-brand top-of-the-line ornamental tree.

WHAT'S THE CATCH?

Traditions are typically built over long periods of time and with some measure of authentic origins. Unless of course we're talking about the recent success of products like The Elf on the Shelf, Mensch on a Bench, or traditions like Administrative Professionals Day. Who are we kidding? The same social pressure that makes Americans spend $20 billion on flowers and candy on the Hallmark-created Valentine's Day could surely be worth a few million bucks when it comes to this fabulous fabricated Wedding Tradition.

WHAT'S THE LIKELIHOOD OF SUCCESS?

Success Rating: 53%

As much as I enjoy the thought of creating a new wedding tradition, The Wedding Tree faces an uphill battle of consumer adoption. Ultimately, I give The Wedding Tree the same shot of success as an actual marriage: a little over fifty percent.

Pardon My Interruption

Contributor: Teresa Day

WHAT IS IT?

A typical corporate working environment is filled with people working in rows of cubicles and in offices. Most people are staring intently at their computer screen, many of whom may even be wearing head-phones to focus or perhaps just to drown out the high-pitched voice of their chatty neighbor. Regardless, anyone who's worked in an office environment knows how frustrating it is to be interrupted when you're busy. If you're fortunate enough to have an office, the door serves as a signal of your availability. If it's open, you're welcome to come in. If it's closed, only enter if you outrank me. But for most employees in open cubicles, there's no way for fellow colleagues to assess your availability without interrupting you to ask. After all, there's a reason stores have open and closed signs. Wouldn't it be nice to assess the availability of coworkers without having to interrupt them?

Introducing Pardon My Interruption, a desk button designed for office workers that lets other employees know whether they can be interrupted at that time. Perhaps the button is affixed to the side of the computer monitor and changes from green (available) to red (unavailable) with the simple press of a button. Have you ever eaten at a Fogo de Chao Brazilian Steakhouse? If so, you likely recall two things: First, that the meat sweats is in fact a real thing, and second, the "button." Each diner has a two-sided button. If the green side is up, waiters know that you want more meat and will continue to serve you. If the red side is up, waiters know to stay away and will not come back until you've flipped your button. It is an effective system that works because of its simplicity.

Pardon My Interruption is the Fogo de Chao meat button of office space availability. The only difference is that in one instance, you're interrupted to eat medium-rare filet mignon, and in the other, you're interrupted to be told your reports are past due.

WHY IS IT NEEDED?

Because it's impossible to tell whether Dave, the quirky guy in finance who always wears over-the-ear-headphones is *actually* busy or not. Work is hard enough, let's take the guessing game out of it. Pardon My Interruption eliminates any doubt about approaching a coworker. Every day, millions of dollars of productivity are lost because people are interrupted while working diligently on a task. Companies will gladly pilot a program that helps fix that.

HOW DOES IT MAKE MONEY?

The key to making this work is to partner with several sizeable companies with tens of thousands of employees. Selling buttons one at a time won't move the needle fast enough. The path to a million dollars goes through large, institutional orders. You need a company like Facebook to order twenty thousand buttons all at once. Once employees get accustomed to using this system, word will spread throughout the corporate community. Before long, Pardon My Interruption will be a staple at every work station.

WHAT'S THE CATCH?

Employees must remember to update their availability status. This may seem simple enough, but it also seems simple to show up to meetings on time, and most employees have a hard enough time doing that.

WHAT'S THE LIKELIHOOD OF SUCCESS?

Success Rating: 65%

I'm bullish on Pardon My Interruption. It is an easy business to start, inexpensive for companies to pilot, and helps to solve a common complaint in the workplace.

DaycAir

Contributor: Nick Madden

WHAT IS IT?

Let me allow Nick, the contributor of this idea, set the scene: I was huddled in the bathroom with my screaming 13-month old on the way from Barcelona to Boston, hiding from the wrath of passengers back at our seats. My daughter had been screaming consistently for about seven hours. Our neighbors were staring daggers at us. The flight attendants were sneering at us. I was about to fight the guy in the next row for shaking his head at us. My wife and I were ready to flush the kid down the toilet or maybe just throw ourselves out the emergency exit door. Sitting there on that grimy toilet seat, I thought about how elegant a solution it would be if everyone on the plane were in the same boat. That is, the answer wasn't a better kid or a private jet. The solution was pooling other parents together so that there was no anxiety about offending other passengers, no need to try to reason with a toddler who doesn't speak English, and no sleeping seniors or busy business travelers - just otherwise despondent parents commiserating on the same flight. Kind of like a flight from LaGuardia to Orlando the Saturday of winter vacation, except planned. Deliberately. By an airline.

Introducing DaycAir, an airline that devotes a portion of every plane to a professionally staffed, sound-proofed daycare seating and play area. Parents sit in front, unburdened by anxiety and alienation. Kids are in back, safe and sound, and free to act their age.

WHY IS IT NEEDED?

Airline travel used to be a special and luxurious experience. Travelers wore their finest clothes and kids grew up dreaming to be a pilot for Pan Am. Well, somewhere along the line things changed, especially for parents traveling with young kids. For them, travel is more closely linked to the ninth circle of hell. Maybe it has something to do with the invasive breast-milk x-ray or the judging looks from business travelers. But one thing is clear – if you've ever traveled with kids, especially those who are unruly and sitting on your lap, you know that the experience is far from special or luxurious. It's simply exhausting. DaycAir solves this problem. Parents say they are willing to spend anything on their kids. Well, you know what else is true? Occasionally they're willing to spend anything to avoid them.

HOW DOES IT MAKE MONEY?

Airlines make money by squeezing as many people onto a plane as possible. As such, travelers on DaycAir would have to pay more as the plane is sacrificing revenue for some of this space and additional staff is required. Fortunately, the kid seats are small, so you can cram them in, and you don't need that much room for play. This is still an airplane after all, not a Dave & Busters. Even if tickets are 2x normal amounts, many parents would still do it in a heartbeat. There's no price tag on sanity.

WHAT'S THE CATCH?

Remember when Hooters tried to start an airline? If big breasts and short shorts can't sell tickets, it might be hard for middle-aged babysitters to. Plus, you need a whole lotta cash to start an airline.

WHAT'S THE LIKELIHOOD OF SUCCESS?

Success Rating: 12-15%

Most airlines allow children from 12 to 15 years old to travel alone, which is exactly the success rating I'm giving to DaycAir. But hey, give it a shot. Maybe you'll be the next Herb Kelleher.

Urine-It to Win-It

Contributor: Scott Moore

WHAT IS IT?

To what is likely the dismay of many women, men love competing at bars. Not just over women, but in whatever games are available. There's a reason that shuffle board, pool, and that admittedly intimidating bar punching bag game are so popular. Bar owners know that certain games help to attract patrons and keep them drinking for longer. These games are also an income stream (foreshadowing pun) for the establishment. Yet, there's one area of most bars that has yet to realize its full potential for monetization – the bathroom.

Introducing Urine-It to Win-It, a competitive bar game for men's urinals. The easiest way to describe this idea is to compare it to a game we're all familiar with - the water gun race at amusement parks. As you recall from your childhood, the objective of the game is to beat your opponents by shooting more water into the target as quickly as possible and popping the balloon or advancing the horse or whatever. The key to winning is accuracy and a consistent stream. You can obviously see where this is going. Urine-It to Win-It applies the same principles of this family-friendly game, but rather than using water, brings it to the watering hole.

While at the urinal, men pee on a target with a sensor that is digitally connected to a scoreboard above the urinal. The more accurate you are and the longer you go, the higher your score. You can compete against yourself or your fellow relievers. The objective is to get the highest score. Like other bar games, Urine-It to Win-It shows the Top 10 scores, so you know where you stand (aside from ready position). It's just like Pop-A-Shot but requires a different a set of balls.

WHY IS IT NEEDED?

The bar industry is very competitive. Bar owners look for any advantage that will get people to drink more and spend more at their establishment. The bathroom is one of the last places that has yet to be properly monetized. Let's be honest, nobody seems to be buying cheap condoms or expired cologne out of those walled vending machines or from bathroom attendants. Urine-It to Win-It is a novelty that will attract patrons (i.e. frat boys) to the bar and encourage them to spend more. Not only by paying for the game itself, but also by incentivizing them to drink more to fill up their bladders in preparation for the next matchup.

Additionally, Urine-It to Win-It helps keep bathrooms clean by encouraging men to aim at a target specifically designed to minimize splashback. All men can agree this is a positive consequence, especially those wearing flip flops.

HOW DOES IT MAKE MONEY?

Urine-It to Win-It sells its product to the approximately 70,000 bars in the U.S. That's a lot of urinals that aren't currently monetized. The product pays for itself from the money required to play and the increase in alcohol sales it drives. I can already envision groups of guys "holding it" so they can line up to compete at the same time.

WHAT'S THE CATCH?

While this product is intended to help keep bathrooms clean, might it have the adverse effect of turning the bathroom into a raucous side show? Intoxicated bargoers may "double up" in one urinal to get a high score. Packs of men may take over the bathroom, blocking other patrons from getting in. Overly competitive frat boys may take to peeing on other players to try and distract them. In its effort to try and monetize bathrooms, Urine-It to Win-It may have unintended consequences that bar owners won't want to deal with.

WHAT'S THE LIKELIHOOD OF SUCCESS?

Success Rating: 79%

Bars recognize the importance of games. It's why I'm always trying to find a bar with Erotic Photo Hunt. Urine-It to Win-It will bring guys to bars and encourage them to spend more while they're there. Without it, bars are (literally) flushing money down the toilet.

Sari I'm Not Sari

Contributor: Reverend Love

WHAT IS IT?

A sari is a female garment worn by Indian women that consists of a drape that is typically wrapped around the waist, with one end draped over the shoulder, baring the midriff. Although let's be clear, this has no resemblance to an American teenager wearing a cropped top shirt that also bares the midriff. Very different looks, I must say. Sarees are traditionally worn by women from the Indian subcontinent and haven't changed a whole lot since they were first worn thousands of years ago. That is until now.

Introducing Sari I'm Not Sari, a garment-to-function fabric business. Sarees that convert into other useful items such as a scarf, hammock, tablecloth, or baby carrier. It is essentially the swiss army knife of garments. It's like how white bed sheets can double as togas, but in reverse. Indian women collect and wear a variety of sarees for different occasions. Sari I'm Not Sari will be the most versatile in her closet. It's a fresh take on an old tradition and you don't need to apologize for it.

WHY IS IT NEEDED?

There are millions of Indian-born residents living in the United States, many of whom are modern Indian-American millennial women. These women want to pay homage and identify with their Indian heritage, but don't feel constrained by the weight of tradition. She needs a sari designed for the modern-day women. A product that has just as many looks and personalities as she does.

Our female readers are undoubtedly familiar with Hermes, a luxury scarf company that touts the many ways you can wear and use their product. Although I'm still not sure that justifies their price point. Regardless, Sari I'm Not Sari is like the Hermes scarf of Indian attire. It's fashionable, functional, and routed in elegance.

HOW DOES IT MAKE MONEY?

It makes money because like most women's fashion, you can charge hundreds

of dollars for pieces of fabric. That Hermes scarf you just paid $400 for? Probably cost them less than $5 to produce. Plus, these sarees will be sold all over the world. With over a billion sari-wearing women out there, you only need to capture a small share to create a million-dollar brand.

WHAT'S THE CATCH?

Sometimes when you try and do too much, you end up doing none of it well. Hence the swiss army knife comparison. Have you ever actually tried to use those tiny little scissors? Yeesh. That could prove to be a challenge with Sari I'm Not Sari. It might do a lot of things, but none of them perfectly. But like the swiss army knife, that didn't stop double-sided belts, transition glasses, and those dreadful zipper pants that turn into shorts, from being multi-million-dollar successes.

WHAT'S THE LIKELIHOOD OF SUCCESS?

Success Rating: 30%

In addition to the Indian-American consumer, the global market for saris is huge. Many a million-dollar business have been built by creating a better mousetrap and that's exactly what Sari I'm Not Sari is. It's another example of fashion meeting function targeted toward the female shopper (see: PKTS).

Nanny Guard

Contributor: Jeff Day

WHAT IS IT?

Every day, families are faced with difficult decisions about childcare. They must weigh the pros and cons of a stay-at-home parent vs. daycare vs. a nanny. Not an easy choice and one that comes with significant financial and lifestyle implications. Let's assume that our make-believe family decided they are going to hire a nanny to take care of their two children. Fantastic! But wait, that's just the beginning. Now it's time to find the *right* nanny. And by right I'm referring to the right level of experience, the right type of personality, and perhaps most importantly, the right level of attractiveness. That's right, one of the hardest decisions related to childcare is whether to bring some young, spirited, attractive woman into your household. It's like putting a slice of fresh-out-of-the-oven cheese pizza in front of someone who is both lactose intolerant and has celiac disease. Sure, that person may not eat the slice, but do you really want them even looking at it?

Introducing Nanny Guard, a caretaker service that only employs qualified, but otherwise unattractive nannies. Nanny Guard adds this critical, but currently overlooked, variable to its screening procedure. Sorry young lady, you seem like a terrific person and a competent caregiver, but you were blessed with beautiful eyes and a slim waistline. This isn't the place for you.

WHY IS IT NEEDED?

Well, for people like Rob Lowe, Jon Gosselin, Robin Williams, Arnold Schwarzenegger, Mick Jagger, David Beckham, Jude Law, Ethan Hawke, Ben Affleck, and Gavin Rossdale for starters (all of whom were accused of sleeping with their nannies). Now, would Nanny Guard have prevented these home-wrecking affairs? Maybe. With perhaps the exception of Schwarzenegger. Regardless, these celebrity examples represent only the tip of the "why would you hire an attractive nanny" iceberg. Raising kids is hard enough as it is. There's no need to make it even harder (pun intended).

HOW DOES IT MAKE MONEY?

Like all services that connect people to jobs, Nanny Guard takes a small percentage of the nanny's annual salary for facilitating the relationship.

However, in the unlikely event of an affair (a clear indication that our value proposition failed), Nanny Guard will issue a full refund. It's the least you could do. Plus, it'll help pay for the divorce lawyers.

WHAT'S THE CATCH?

Those pesky things called employee discrimination laws. Remember when Abercrombie & Fitch got sued for only hiring attractive people to work in their stores? This is like the same thing but in reverse. Although if you ask me, it's about time good-looking people finally got discriminated against.

WHAT'S THE LIKELIHOOD OF SUCCESS?

Success Rating: 16-18%

It only felt appropriate to give this business the same chances of success as the age of consent. Unless that country is Nigeria, where the chance of success would then be 11. Yikes. Nanny Guard is a funny concept to imagine, but largely impractical because of the legal and ethical barriers to adoption.

Shower Stick-It

Contributor: Teresa Day

WHAT IS IT?

Let's face it ladies – your hair, while beautiful, makes a mess! My wife, bless her heart, collects her excess hair and "sticks it" to the wall of the shower to avoid clogging the drain. Then she collects this lovely pile of hair with her hands or a tissue and throws it away. Voila, it disappears! It's like a magic trick – if only magic was meant to disgust both the magician and the audience (in this case, the partner or roommate who share the shower). There must be a better way for women (and all you fellas with great flow) to more effectively collect and dispose of excess hair while showering.

Introducing Shower Stick-It, a tear-away pad for the shower that collects excess hair and is easily detached and thrown away after each use. It's like a big post-it note, but instead of collecting a list of to-dos, it collects strands of hair. The pad (consisting of individual tear-away sheets) sticks to the wall with water-resistant adhesive. Each sheet has an adhesive that collects hair and is effortlessly ripped off and tossed away. This is not a complicated product nor one that requires advanced technology. It is a simple solution to an everyday problem in almost all households.

WHY IS IT NEEDED?

Look, it's not a question of whether excess hair exists. If you are a woman, or have ever shared a shower with a woman, you understand this problem. The only question is where the hair goes. Down the drain or collected and discarded. Just like women expect men to put the seat down after peeing, men should be able to walk into a shower without it feeling like the drop-off center for Locks of Love (which, by the way, is a wonderful charity to consider if you're planning to cut off 10 inches of hair).

Women want a more convenient way to discard loose hair and men simply want to shower in peace. We're all familiar with the expression Happy Wife, Happy Life, right? Well here's a new one for you: Happy Husband, Happy... Nothing. Yep, that's right. Sorry gentlemen, but there's still no correlation between your happiness and... anything, really. Regardless, Shower Stick-It should be a household staple, particularly if you want a *happy* household. :)

HOW DOES IT MAKE MONEY?

Shower Stick-It is a household item that should be sold at every Bed Bath and Beyond and similar household retailers. If it were being pitched on *Shark Tank*, Lori Greiner, "The Queen of QVC," would be all over it. This product not only solves a need in every household with a longhaired inhabitant, but in every *shower* within said households. And public showers too! More showers equal more sheets. More sheets equal more pads. And more pads equal more millions.

WHAT'S THE CATCH?

Unless women start shaving their head ala Demi Moore in *GI Jane*, or science finds a way to eliminate hair from falling out, there will always be excess hair and a need to dispose of it. If successful, Shower Stick-It could face significant levels of competition as the product itself is not very defensible.

WHAT'S THE LIKELIHOOD OF SUCCESS?

Success Rating: 83%

I'm bullish on Shower Stick-It. The market is huge, the problem it's addressing is common and consistent, and the product is simple and easy to master. It's an improved solution to a commonly over-looked issue. Plus, my wife came up with it so she must be on to something.

Secret Sender

Contributor: Jeff Day

WHAT IS IT?

What are among Americans most-loved activities (besides dealing with a completely incomprehensible system of measurement and pretending you're from Canada when traveling)? Murder mysteries and receiving cards in the mail. Well, what if you could combine these two seemingly distinct interests into one business idea? Minus the whole murder part, of course.

Introducing Secret Sender, a service that sends mystery greeting cards on your behalf to a recipient of your choosing. Via a digital platform, users select a card, write a note, and enter a recipient's mailing address. A few days later, a card is delivered for you. Presto. Easy like Sunday morning (shout out to Lionel Richie). But that's not all, right? Of course not.

When a person receives a card from Secret Sender, the following two-phased reaction will occur:

Phase 1 (Delight): Aw, this is great. I love getting mail. It was so nice to get a birthday card from...

Phase 2 (Confusion): ...Wait. Who's this from? Secret Sender? I'm so confused.

That's right. When you receive a card from Secret Sender, you don't know who it's from! A good ole' whodunnit? (besides Adnan Syed and Steven Avery, of course). But what if you want to know the sender's identity? You've got to pay it forward and send a new card to someone else. Yes, you read that correctly! You'll be able to unlock the identify of your secret sender once you become a secret sender yourself. It's a self-perpetuating business model. One card starts a never-ending cycle of cards (and therefore revenue). It's like that movie *Pay it Forward*, but *with* greeting cards and *without* Haley Joel Osment (he might be a good spokesperson and is likely available for cheap).

You're gamifying the card giving experience. In doing so, you're putting smiles on faces and money into your pockets. Is this the ever-elusive win-win scenario? I'm not sure, but this is Secret Sender.

WHY IS IT NEEDED?

If you've got a mailbox, people that you care about, and a connection to the internet, this idea is for you. Not Gen Z, though. That generation is a lost cause. Secret Sender combines the latest in technology with the nostalgia of snail mail. In today's digital society, receiving a card is more meaningful than ever. Plus, who doesn't love a good mystery?

HOW DOES IT MAKE MONEY?

Users pay a fee that includes the cost of the card and shipping. This service won't be any more expensive than buying and shipping a card yourself. And definitely a lot cheaper than Papyrus cards. Good grief. There's also an opportunity for add-on services. You want to include a $50 gift card inside your card? No problem, that will only cost you $55.

WHAT'S THE CATCH?

This might be a ponzi scheme.

WHAT'S THE LIKELIHOOD OF SUCCESS?

Success Rating: 74%

I'm bullish on Secret Sender. This business isn't a long-term play. It's a novelty service. Get in. Make money. Get out. The biggest challenge is generating cost-effective awareness to get the dominos to start falling. But with a smart seeding plan and the support of a viral campaign, this business could quickly make a million dollars.

iBandaid

Contributor: Caitlin Hess

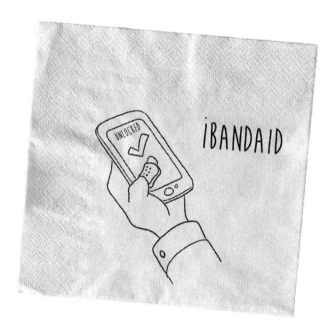

WHAT IS IT?

Did you know that Band-Aid is a brand, not a type of product? The product is actually called an adhesive bandage, but Band-Aid, the brand, became so synonymous with the category that we often refer to all adhesive bandages as "band-aids." Another example like this is Kleenex. The product type is facial tissue; Kleenex is simply a brand of them. Back to adhesive bandages, or "band-aids." Over the years, companies have innovated on the traditional bandage to stand out from competitors. Everything from decorative, to waterproof, to flexible bandages are now readily available. They've thought of everything except the most important kind of bandage there is – the one that lets you operate your touch-screen phone even when your thumb is covered.

Introducing iBandaid, a touchscreen-capable adhesive bandage. In layman's terms, it's a "band-aid" that can still read your fingerprint through the adhesive or protective material. This enables you to seamlessly use touchscreen and fingerprint enabled devices while at the same time treating your boo-boo. Look, I'm not about to explain the technology that allows this to happen (mostly because I don't fully understand it), but the good news is that it already exists. Gloves have been using this technology for years. Apparel companies realized that consumers were unwilling to separate themselves from their phones just because it was cold outside. How *dare* we expose our finger tips to freezing temps while scrolling through our Insta feed!

iBandaid isn't developing a new technology, it's simply applying it to a different type of product. A cut on your thumb should never prevent you from easily accessing your phone without the added effort of typing in a four-digit code, now should it?

WHY IS IT NEEDED?

Unlike taking medicine, you don't often think about the side effects of applying an adhesive bandage to one of your fingers. It doesn't cause drowsiness, suicidal thoughts, or temporary blindness. It can lead to something far worse: touchscreen separation anxiety. This condition may not yet be recognized by the medical board, but quite honestly, it doesn't feel that farfetched.

The reality is that before long, almost all screens will be touchscreen enabled. Prior to this revolution, it was never a big deal to create a barrier between your fingerprint and a digital device (unless perhaps you were in the CIA). That's no longer the case. We're not all Jason Bourne, but gosh, not being able to access an app with fingerprint verification often feels like a matter of national security.

The need for iBandaid stretches well beyond just one's phone. Paper cuts aren't going away anytime soon, and fingerprint verification will only become more prevalent. An injury so small (yet surprisingly painful) should never have consequences so large.

HOW DOES IT MAKE MONEY?

The business depends on people's unrelenting addiction to their digital devices as well as the continued emergence of fingerprint-enabled devices. It also assumes that people will continue to be clumsy and cut themselves (feels like a safe bet). A phone is one thing. But when unlocking your car or house is based on fingerprint recognition, people may be willing to pay a premium to do so unencumbered by an old-fashioned bandage.

WHAT'S THE CATCH?

Besides the fact that it's probably prohibitively expensive to embed touchscreen-capable technology into a disposable bandage? Well, other than that, it doesn't help that most fingerprint verifications, including unlocking your phone, allow you to program multiple fingerprints. So, unless you happen to simultaneously cut all your fingers, chances are good you can still access your apps without too much difficulty. Darn you, Apple, you've thought of everything.

WHAT'S THE LIKELIHOOD OF SUCCESS?

Success Rating: 25%

iBandaid may seem silly now, but perhaps that's because it's ahead of its time. In the meantime, I'll stick with you, Band-Aid.

Spiked Cubes

Contributor: Leslie Day

WHAT IS IT?

Anyone that enjoys a good cocktail understands the importance of ice. How much to use? What size and shape? With what water quality? These questions may seem trivial, but they are critical in crafting the perfect cocktail. While the ice does a stellar job chilling the drink, it also dilutes the alcohol. And no one likes watered down cocktails (that is, unless you're like me and prefer to drink your whiskey once the ice has melted into it to avoid the embarrassment of coughing while taking the first sip. But I digress). The point is that while cocktails have exploded in popularity and craftsmanship, the ice used to cool them down hasn't changed in a long, long time (dare I say it... since the "ice age"). It's time that cocktails were finally made with ice that *enhances* the drinking experience.

Introducing Spiked Cubes, a brand of alcohol-infused ice cubes available in different liquors and flavors to compliment your favorite drink. These boozy balls (a close second for the name of this idea) not only chill your drink, but add more alcohol and enhance the taste. No dilution here! Need vodka cubes to cool down that refreshing Greyhound? No problem. How about a handful of gin cubes for your Tom Collins? We've got you covered. And that's not all. Spiked Cubes are also available in popular cocktail flavors such as Mai Tai, Margarita, Mojito, and Moscow Mule (and you thought a copper mug was "basic").

Spiked Cubes will forever change the way you tip 'em back. Cheers!

WHY IS IT NEEDED?

You know what makes a specialty cocktail even more special (besides the aforementioned copper mug)? Fancy ice. Spiked Cubes will become so popular that it will make classic cocktails using regular ice seem, well, a little less special. An Old-Fashioned using water cubes... just feels old. A High Ball... more like low ball. And a Manhattan with plain old ice... well shoot, that becomes known simply as a Cleveland (sorry, Cleveland).

HOW DOES IT MAKE MONEY?

Spiked Cubes would not only be available nationwide in grocery and liquor stores, but also sold directly to thousands of bars and restaurants across the country. Cocktails made with Spiked Cubes would command a higher price point which incentivizes these establishments to serve them.

WHAT'S THE CATCH?

First, there's that pesky thing called science – our domestic freezers are no match for the freezing points of most alcohols. The half-baked portion of this book is confident there is a way to make alcoholic ice cubes, but the other half isn't quite as sure. Second, and potentially more troublesome, is the liability of making cocktails even more alcoholic. Young people can't hold their liquor when it's being diluted with water, nevertheless when it's filled with watermelon vodka cubes. I'm not sure I want my daughter growing up in a world with alcoholic ice cubes. A father has enough to worry about already.

WHAT'S THE LIKELIHOOD OF SUCCESS?

Success Rating: 21%

This one was obvious – I had to equate Spiked Cube's likelihood of success to that of the legal drinking age. The billion-dollar drinking market is ready, waiting, and thirsty for something new. We just need a few scientists spending less time focused on quantum physics and a little more time focused on getting us all drunk.

Seasons Change

Contributor: Ryan Keller

WHAT IS IT?

There are a lot of wonderful things about city living. One thing that isn't so wonderful, however, is lack of affordable living space. Apartments are not only pricey, but are often accompanied by messy roommates, noisy neighbors, and perhaps most importantly, limited closet space. Finding room for all your clothes is a daunting task, even for the most sophisticated packers. What makes matters worse is that in most places, items are only worn for a specific period of the year. While that J. Crew cardigan is a winter staple, it spends the rest of the year lying dormant - taking up invaluable closet space and collecting dust. Wouldn't it be nice if your closet only had to make room for clothes you're actually wearing?

Introducing Seasons Change, a seasonal closet storage service for urban residents with limited space. Seasons Change (I'm particularly proud of this name) is a turn-key service that collects, stores, cleans, and returns items of clothing based on the season. Let's take Lauren as an example. Lauren is a twenty-something living in Manhattan. She shares an 800 sq. ft. apartment with 3 girls and has a closet smaller than most Soul Cycle lockers. As winter turns to spring, Lauren hires Seasons Change to pick-up sweaters, heavy coats, and clunky boots, all of which were piled up under her bed or in a dirty storage unit to make room for her summer attire. Ahh, the relief. While Lauren spends the next several months basking in the delight of rooftop pool parties and a more livable bedroom, her clothes are being professionally maintained and prepped in climate-controlled storage. When the days begin to shorten, and the air turns brisk, Seasons Change returns Lauren's winter items in exchange for swimsuits, short shorts, and memories of fleeting summer romance.

WHY IS IT NEEDED?

Seasons Change (again, what a name, right?) solves a very real problem for urban dwellers, primarily fashionable females who have a lot of clothing, but not a lot of space. And don't worry, we're not ignoring all the fashion-forward men out there either (See: Suns Out Buns Out). You're not alone! There are millions of people who suffer from closet-shortages (suddenly this sounds like a medical infomercial). Back to the point, Seasons Change not only frees up physical space,

but equally important, also returns clothing ready-to-wear. We all know that a wool sweater hastily packed away for 8 months in the bottom of a drawer can have a funky whiff to it. Seasons Change is here to help. Not necessarily with the whole summer romance thing, though. You're still on your own for that.

HOW DOES IT MAKE MONEY?

Consumers pay a small fee based on the number of items and length of storage. Seasons Change can also offer complimentary services such as dry cleaning to generate additional sources of revenue. Operationally, the model is relatively simple and cheap to execute. In fact, Seasons Change can partner with apartment and condo buildings (by offering a discounted rate) to get large volume at a single location.

WHAT'S THE CATCH?

Expansion is limited by climate. For example, Seasons Change doesn't work so well in San Diego or Tampa Bay because, let's face it, the seasons don't *really* change. At least not enough to justify this service. It also assumes consumers are willing to forego access to certain items for extended periods of time. What happens if you're planning to take a Caribbean vacation during the middle of winter? Can you have items returned mid-storage? Would this limit interest in the service? All questions to be answered in the second half of the baking process.

WHAT'S THE LIKELIHOOD OF SUCCESS?

Success Rating: 72%

Seasons Change is a winner. And not just because I think it's a great name (although that certainly doesn't hurt). Young adults continue to value convenience and are willing to pay for services that make their lives just a little bit easier. Its success rating is also in honor of the season that never goes out of style: 72 and sunny.

FaceSpace

Contributors: Neil Patel & Chuck Feerick

WHAT IS IT?

We are exposed to around 4,000 to 10,000 advertisements every single day. The average person doesn't even recognize the brands they interact with daily. Heck, I'm sitting at a desk writing on a Logitech keyboard, powered by a Lenovo laptop, projecting on a Dell monitor, all while my Apple iPhone plays music on a Bose Mini. As individuals, we're essentially walking billboards for the brands we wear and interact with. And brands recognize the power of social influence. It's why a headphone company partnered with a hip-hop star (Dr. Dre); why a tequila company partnered with a famous actor (George Clooney); and why a shoe company partnered with a basketball star (Michael Jordan). While these are extreme examples, the logic holds true for all of us. We're all influencers. Consequently, what we choose to promote has inherent value. And nothing is more visible to those we interact with then what's on our face. Don't worry, I'm not advocating for face tattoos. But what if I told you there are over a billion people wearing something every single day that *isn't* branded...yet.

Introducing FaceSpace, a company that sells advertising on the pollution masks that people wear in China. For those keeping track, this is the second idea presented in the book that is targeted toward the Chinese market. In China, pollution masks are worn every day by everyone. Said differently, that's over a billion vacant billboards - a lot of valuable media real estate. FaceSpace will sell advertising on these masks and charge different rates based on the social influence of the individual. In fact, companies might even be able to write off some of the advertising costs as corporate social responsibility.

WHY IS IT NEEDED?

Unless you're a celebrity, people can rarely profit off their own personal billboard. FaceSpace changes that by leveraging the scale of an everyday accessory with the insatiable need for manufacturers to advertise. Does the world need more advertisements? Of course not. But is it a viable untapped branding opportunity? It just might be.

HOW DOES IT MAKE MONEY?

This could work in a variety of ways. Remember, this is only half-baked. But the basic premise is that individuals "own" the space on their mask and can choose to rent it out. Individuals will command different prices, depending on their pre-determined level of social influence (which is dynamic and changes over time). FaceSpace takes a percentage of the deal for brokering the transaction. This could get complicated quite quickly, but you get the idea.

WHAT'S THE CATCH?

I'll repeat: have you ever tried launching a business in China? I didn't think so. There are a host of barriers to conducting business overseas, particularly in Asia. Not that I know or understand any of them, but I can only assume that's the case. So, while the consumer demand may exist, you may find the business can't get the oxygen it needs to survive (yep, did it again).

WHAT'S THE LIKELIHOOD OF SUCCESS?

Success Rating: 50%

By now you know my rule for businesses operating in Asia. Regardless of the strength of the idea, it's a coin-flip at best. FaceSpace allows consumers the opportunity to treat their face like a billboard and decide whether to profit from it. It's modern day media. And it scares the hell out of me.

Mow-to-Go

Contributor: Ryan E.

WHAT IS IT?

People take great pride in the appearance of their freshly cut lawn. And I'm speaking about the people who cut it themselves, not the privileged folk who pay their way to a perfectly manicured front yard. In fact, I know a guy that doesn't even like the taste of beer, but cracks open a fresh can of Budweiser every time he's finished mowing his lawn because "it just feels right." Now, that's American. Perhaps this pleasure is, in part, derived from the fact that mowing your lawn is a bit of a time-consuming nuisance. This is especially true if you don't want the grass clippings left behind on the lawn, in which case you must stop countless times to transfer the clippings from the mower's container into paper bags for the curb. What if there was a way to remove this step and make lawnmowing just a little bit easier?

Introducing Mow-to-Go, a lawnmower, or attachment, that collects grass clippings directly into a disposable, environmentally friendly paper bag. Transferring clippings from one container to another is downright silly. Mow-to-Go collects clippings directly into a throw-away bag so that when it's full, you simply detach, tie-up, and take it to the curb. Can you imagine having a garbage can in your kitchen that you transfer to a *different* bag to throw out? That would be pure madness. Yet, it's essentially what your husband (or in some cases, wife) is doing every other Saturday afternoon. Mow-to-Go makes disposing grass clippings just a little bit easier - and don't worry, you don't need to admit that to your spouse.

WHY IS IT NEEDED?

Nowadays, lawnmowers practically cut the grass themselves. They're self-propelled, have effective cutting blades, and plenty of horsepower. Heck, these things even have All-Wheel Drive systems. But unless you're cutting the greens at Augusta National, you don't really care. Most guys just want a reliable mower that helps them cross off an item on their weekend to-do list. And perhaps get a two-hour break from the wife and kids. The point is that all the mowers on the market can effectively cut grass a couple of inches. What's needed is a mower that makes it easier to *dispose* of said grass.

HOW DOES IT MAKE MONEY?

Mow-to-Go is another classic razor blade model (see: One and Done). Users will re-purchase bags as they use them. Aside from the core business model, Mow-to-Go must implement a creative marketing strategy to gain ground in the competitive lawncare market. This business must tap into the uniquely competitive dynamics of suburban neighborhood living. All of you home-owners know exactly what I'm talking about. That's why Mow-to-Go will give away its product for free to all the nicest looking yards in the neighborhood. Neighbors already look to them for inspiration (or judgment). Once they see Mr. Jones pushing around a Mow-to-Go, rest assured they'll be heading to Lowe's to pick up one themselves.

WHAT'S THE CATCH?

The disposable bag needs to be cheap enough to make it affordable, but strong enough to prevent rocks from flying through it and cutting down something far more precious than the grass. After all, you shouldn't have to wear a cup to mow your lawn.

WHAT'S THE LIKELIHOOD OF SUCCESS?

Success Rating: 40%

Self-driving autonomous lawnmowers aren't far away, but until then, Mow-to-Go helps you achieve the true American dream: having a better-looking lawn than your next-door neighbor.

Good Vibes

Contributor: Teresa Day

WHAT IS IT?

Today there is a secondhand market for practically everything. Want to sell your used car? Go to CarMax. Want to trade in your iPhone? Go to Gazelle. Want to see what your old clothing is worth? Go to Buffalo Exchange. These companies exist because people want to get value for items they no longer use and they cater to those who cannot afford to buy everything new or simply prefer a good deal. The minute you drive a new car off the lot it loses approximately 10 percent of its value. The car hasn't changed, but it's no longer "new" and thus worth less. Despite the emergence of secondhand marketplaces across almost every consumer facing industry, there isn't a trusted reseller of one of the most common- ly owned, yet infrequently used, product categories out there: sex toys.

Introducing Good Vibes, a marketplace for secondhand sex toys (pun intended). Good Vibes is an authorized buyer and reseller that purchases, sanitizes, re-packages, and sells sex toys and lingerie. The sex industry can be filled with unscrupulous entities, but Good Vibes is a trusted and respected reseller. Remember when you had to scalp concert or sporting event tickets from some shady guy outside the stadium until StubHub and SeatGeek came along? Well, Good Vibes is the StubHub of vibrators!

Good Vibes purchases sex toys and lingerie and does all the dirty work for you (more intended puns). Good Vibes buys from people who no longer, or perhaps never did, use the sex toys in their possession. The items are sanitized and resold to individuals who do want to use them at a significantly discounted rate versus the original price. After all, while a car might lose 10% of its value when its driven off the lot, the depreciation of sex toys is probably much steeper.

WHY IS IT NEEDED?

Every year, millions of unused sex toys and lingerie go to waste. The biggest culprit? Bachelorette parties. Many women come home with a box filled with vibrating pleasure sticks, but simply don't have the need to use them, or at least not *all* of them. And unlike most items you receive and don't intend to use, you can't return sex toys. For good reason, I guess.

Sex toys are expensive, often unused, and unreturnable. For many women, receiving a sex toy is like getting a $50 gift card for Long John Silvers. Sure, you've thought about trying it out from time to time, but ultimately it sits in the back of some drawer out of plain sight. After all, what would your parents think if they discovered you safe harboring a gift card to Long John Silvers? The disappointment on their faces...

Don't get me wrong, there are also plenty of women who *do* want to use sex toys, which is important because they are the buyers. These women enjoy experimenting with a variety of sex toys but are tired of paying the exorbitant prices. Good Vibes provides a solution.

HOW DOES IT MAKE MONEY?

Good Vibes purchases an item, marks it up, and resells it. This business operates the same way as other authorized resellers. The products might be a little more unusual, but the business principles remain the same.

WHAT'S THE CATCH?

More like what you hope you *don't* catch, if you know what I mean.

Many people will find this idea rather off-putting. Women who aren't using their sex toys will be more than happy to sell them, but it remains to be seen whether there is a big enough market for women who want to buy them. After all, most women try to avoid sloppy seconds.

WHAT'S THE LIKELIHOOD OF SUCCESS?

Success Rating: 69%

I mean, c'mon. I had to, right? If Marky Mark can find a way to turn Good Vibrations into a million-dollar song, you can surely find a way to turn it into a million-dollar business.

Baby Swiffer

Contributor: Kevin Hess

WHAT IS IT?

Prior to learning how to walk, infants spend most of their time making a mess and crawling around on the floor. For the baby, crawling is merely a way to get from point A to point B. He is unfazed by the type or cleanliness of the surface because let's face it, he doesn't really know what it is he's doing anyway. In other words, a crawling baby is essentially an unproductive broom, just pushing stuff around the floor with its protruding belly. But what if there was a way to turn that unhelpful sweeper into something more useful?

Introducing Baby Swiffer, an attachment for baby clothing that allows infants to clean the floors as they crawl. Baby Swiffer is a detachable and disposable pad that affixes to the front of an infant's clothing. As the baby crawls across the floor, the pad collects excess dirt, dust, hair, and particles of food. The pad can be removed at any time and tossed in the garbage. The baby is doing household chores without complaining or asking for any money! You're welcome, parents!

WHY IS IT NEEDED?

Babies are pretty much useless, demanding our full attention and giving us almost nothing in return. Eventually, of course, they come around but for a while, they're mostly selfish little creatures we're simply trying to keep alive. Wouldn't it be nice if they had a way to give back? To provide any sort of value to the parents trying to raise them?

Let's not kid ourselves (pun intended), Baby Swiffer isn't really needed. But neither is half the stuff you buy when you have a kid. At least this might pick some Cheerios up off the floor.

HOW DOES IT MAKE MONEY?

Chances are you have a Swiffer in your house or have at least used one. Swiffer doesn't necessarily make money from the broom stick, but it generates profits because users must purchase disposable cleaning pads. In this case, your baby is the broom stick. It's even self-propelled!

Baby Swiffer sells a variety of disposable cleaning pads that consumers must re-purchase after use. That is, until the baby learns to walk...

WHAT'S THE CATCH?

The idea of treating your child like a household appliance may seem undesirable to some, especially those that want to be thought of as "good parents," per se. In fact, most parents try hard to keep their infants *away* from germs and not devise methods to have babies collect them. But the reality is that Baby Swiffer helps *protect* your child from germs since the cleaning pad acts as a barrier between the floor and the clothing the toddler is wearing. Plus, by the time you're raising a third child, you stop caring about germs anyway.

WHAT'S THE LIKELIHOOD OF SUCCESS?

Success Rating: 40%

There is no denying that Baby Swiffer is a bit of a wacky idea. But it only takes a few funny videos of adorable infants unknowingly cleaning the hardwood kitchen floor to create a social media phenomenon. Just be willing to accept the fact that you'll likely never become president of your school's PTA.

Bet Roulette

Contributor: Lars Weborg

WHAT IS IT?

In case you haven't noticed, sports betting is big business. The essence of which is to bet on the outcome of an event that has yet to take place. Professional bettors would argue it's a game of skill. Amateur bettors would tell you it's mostly for fun. But finding the opportunity to gamble can be difficult. It's dependent on being in Las Vegas, Atlantic City, or depositing your money into a sketchy online sportsbook headquartered in the Bahamas. What if there was a way to make sports betting available all the time to everyone, completely detached from the outcome of *future* events?

Introducing Bet Roulette, an online and mobile-based gambling platform where you bet on games that have already occurred. You know the matchup, but you don't know the year. It's low-stakes gambling meets sports history. Let me explain. You hit a button that says randomize and get a matchup of the Boston Red Sox versus the New York Yankees. The Yankees odds are -105 and Red Sox are +105 given the historical win/loss record between the two teams (if you don't know what that means this idea probably isn't for you). In this example, the Yankees and Red Sox have played against each other 2,231 times, of which the Yankees have won 1,200 times (54%). The odds are therefore a reflection of that history. You decide your wager and which team to bet on. Bet Roulette isn't a casino so you're not betting against the house. Instead, you're betting against someone taking the other team. Once the bet is locked, Bet Roulette reveals which matchup you've wagered on. In this case, it reveals you just bet on game 7 of the 2003 American League Championship Series in which the Yankees prevailed 6-5 in extra innings. The person who bet on the Yankees wins the bet.

Here's the kicker: in addition to the outcome of the bet, Bet Roulette also provides a concise recap of the game and a video highlight. This is the key. This gambling platform adds incremental value beyond serving as a skill-less mechanism to win or lose money. Bet Roulette is just as much about enjoying sports history with friends as it is about making or losing a few bucks.

Like the popular game Catch Phrase, Bet Roulette can be set to randomize, or players can select a specific category. Playing in random offers the opportunity to bet on matchups across the sporting universe. Everything from Sampras vs. Agassi, to Ohio State vs. Michigan, to Tiger vs. Phil. Alternatively, if you're a big fan of baseball (one of the few that remain), you can choose to bet on matchups only within that sport. And unlike an *actual* baseball game, this will take less than 4.5 hours to complete.

WHY IS IT NEEDED?

Quite simply, people love to gamble, especially against friends. It's why every year millions of dollars are bet on whether the coin toss during the Superbowl will be heads or tails. This platform is intended for the type of people who are betting on the coin toss, not the professional betters seeking an edge. It's really just a form of (pretty cheap) entertainment targeted toward groups of dudes and their sports-loving female friends. Let's be honest, guys love sports and making bets with each other. Bet Roulette knocks it out of the park. A homerun, if you will.

HOW DOES IT MAKE MONEY?

Unlike most sportsbooks, Bet Roulette doesn't take a vig. For those less familiar with betting lingo, the vigorish, or vig, is the amount charged by a bookmaker for taking a bet from a gambler. Bookmakers use this practice to make money from their wagers regardless of the outcome. Bet Roulette doesn't take a vig in part because it makes the service more attractive to betters (they keep all the money) and in part because it allows the company to avoid federal regulation (or so I believe). Instead, Bet Roulette makes money the boring way, by selling advertising on the site.

WHAT'S THE CATCH?

In case you weren't following, Bet Roulette is purely a game of chance.

There is no skill. You're placing a bet without any competitive edge. Remember the movie *Back To The Future 2*? Old Biff gives the Grays Sports Almanac to his 1955 alter ego, enabling young Biff to become a millionaire by betting on games that already happened. This is sort of like that, except not at all. You've got the sports Almanac, but you don't know which game you're betting on. Do people really want to risk their money on a game of pure chance?

WHAT'S THE LIKELIHOOD OF SUCCESS?

Success Rating: 22.2%

I would love to say this idea has even odds of making it because it would fit the narrative quite nicely, but like any oddsmaker, I must be realistic. Therefore, this idea's likelihood of success is opening with a line of 7/2 (which yes, translates to 22.2%).

Plus One

Contributor: Blake Holman

WHAT IS IT?

Growing up, our parents taught us not to talk to strangers. But they never said anything about not *hiring* strangers. In fact, we do it all the time. We use Angie's List to hire contractors and Care.com to hire babysitters. Heck, Jews even hire professional hype dancers for bar mitzvahs. We hire strangers for many reasons, whether that be to fix a toilet or care for a child. Plus, activities are only as fun as the people you do them with. Hence why those paid dancers are the first ones on the dance floor when the Hava Nagila starts playing. A night out can range from boring to spectacular largely depending on who is there (and how many shots of Fireball you've had). What if there was a way to hire strangers to enhance a wide variety of social situations?

Introducing Plus One, an escort service to hire non-sexual social companions. Plus One is a marketplace for people who can be hired for their social specialties. For example, you may hire someone who's smart to be on your trivia team; someone who's good looking to be your wingman; someone who's athletic to play in your intramural sports league; someone who's gay to attend your bachelorette party, or simply someone who's funny to join you and your friends for an evening out. Every social companion would be searchable by their specialty and have transparent ratings and reviews. It's like shopping on Amazon but instead of buying a toaster oven, you're looking for a well-read intellectual to invite to book club. Life is about the people you share it with.

WHY IS IT NEEDED?

We often think of escorts or companions with regard to romantic situations. While Plus One could be your wedding date (hence the name), its purpose goes well beyond one-to-one companionship. That said, it does remind me of the plot of the 2004 romcom, *The Wedding Date*, starring Debra Messing. In the movie, her character hires a male escort as a wedding date. Because it's a Hollywood fantasy, they inevitably fall in love. In real life, this decision would have more likely resulted in Debra Messing starring as

the missing person on an episode of Dateline 20/20. I guess that's not really a selling point for Plus One. Let's move on...

The point is that there are many occasions that would be enhanced with the presence of some person(s) with a specific set of social attributes. We've been paying for hard skills for years. It's time soft skills got their due.

HOW DOES IT MAKE MONEY?

Like any successful marketplace, Plus One is dependent on having enough to sell (in this case, people) and enough people that want to buy. It's for this reason that most dating apps never make it. The marketplace isn't balanced. If Plus One finds its equilibrium, the business profits by taking a percentage of every social connection.

WHAT'S THE CATCH?

The problem is that despite its pure intentions, it still feels kind of sketchy, right? It only takes one bad apple to spoil the bunch. Alas, even if you're able to get past the safety concerns, it's unclear whether people are willing to pay for it. An obstacle to any business that requires an individual's time is that it is expensive. In this case, the juice may not be worth the squeeze (I felt compelled to get one more oddly placed fruit reference in).

WHAT'S THE LIKELIHOOD OF SUCCESS?

Success Rating: 14%

In theory, Plus One plays a practical role that may be worth paying for. In reality, hiring a stranger to hang out still seems pretty weird.

Boats & Bubbles

Contributor: Jeff Day

WHAT IS IT?

People love drinking champagne. People love being on boats. And people *really* love drinking champagne *while* on a boat. I dare say the whole is greater than the sum of its parts (just made that up myself). Yet despite this perfect pairing, there is one component that while strong, presents a glaring weakness: glass. Anyone who has experienced being on a boat when glass breaks appreciates the unpleasant severity of this scenario.

Introducing Boats & Bubbles (B&B), the first and only champagne developed specifically for boating enthusiasts. B&B is champagne packaged in plastic bottles so that passengers can imbibe without any of the safety concerns associated with glass containers. If you're anything like me, you're already starting to visualize this nautical-themed bottle. The cork is encircled by what looks like a miniature orange life ring while the neck of the bottle is wrapped in "safety rope." And here's the kicker – the label is detachable and designed for users to handwrite a message on the back (like a postcard). So, after drinking the champagne, people can fulfill their childhood fantasy of sending out to sea an *actual* message in a bottle. How fun is that? Somewhere out there Sting is smiling.

WHY IS IT NEEDED?

Not many of the ideas presented in this book are inspired by the notion of safety, but Boats & Bubbles very much is. Not long ago I was on a party boat and, to the surprise of no one who's ever been on a party boat, a bottle of champagne broke and injured a fellow passenger. Somehow drinking champagne on a boat isn't quite as much fun when you've got shards of glass stuck in your feet.

HOW DOES IT MAKE MONEY?

Ultimately the boating community needs to embrace Boats & Bubbles as the only champagne bottle permitted on watercraft. The best place to start: cruise ships. Big business and an industry that values passenger safety above all else. All aboard!

Plus, you'll litter the sea (literally) with messages in these bottles. It's like guerrilla marketing, but for the ocean. I guess we need a new name for that.

WHAT'S THE CATCH?

There's probably a good "catch of the day" sea reference I should make here, but I'll spare you. In reality, the catch is that I'm not sure if it's possible to package champagne in a plastic container. The high pressure of the contents is the reason why glass is used. But there must be a way to use high-grade plastic, right? Look, I'm no scientist. I'm just a guy who wants to be able to pop bottles out on the open water without fear of walking on broken glass. First Sting, now Annie Lennox. And quite possibly a lot of readers who have no idea what I'm talking about.

WHAT'S THE LIKELIHOOD OF SUCCESS?

Success Rating: 22%

I'm a product marketer so naturally I love the potential of this product and brand. However, I'd be hard-pressed to give it a high success rating if I don't know whether it can be produced. And if you're wondering if I spent a lot of time trying to determine that, I think you already know the answer.

PKTS

Contributor: Aaron Huang

WHAT IS IT?

As men, we take for granted several things when it comes to our attire. Free from the pressure of wearing constrictive footwear and undergarments, our outfits have two overwhelming benefits: they are generally easy to pee in and virtually everything we wear has pockets. Women don't have it so easy. In fact, 8 out of 10 women say that a cute cocktail dress with pockets is one of the most coveted wardrobe staples of the 21st century. Well ladies, what if there was a brand that made it easier to find fashionable outfits with the convenience of pockets?

Introducing PKTS, an apparel company that exclusively sells women's clothing with pockets. Specifically, this company focuses on items that *don't* commonly have pockets. Items like dresses, rompers, workout pants, and so on. Solely focused on solving an unmet need in the women's clothing marketplace, this company is tackling it one pocket at a time. Its focused message is inspired by the men's shirt company, UNTUCKit. Its entire premise is to sell men's collared shirts that are meant to be worn untucked. If UNTUCKit can create a multi-million-dollar business selling untucked shirts to men, surely PKTS can create a successful business selling fashionable apparel with pockets to women.

WHY IS IT NEEDED?

Women often lament the fact that what they're wearing doesn't have any pockets. So-much-so that the following conversation is not uncommon:

"Oh my gosh, I love that dress!"

"Thanks! It has pockets!" [cue girl putting both sets of hands in the pockets to really drive the point home]

Women are accustomed to pocketless apparel and this business isn't trying to change that. But like an LBD (that's "little black dress" for our male readers), every woman should have at least one item from PKTS in her closet, perhaps one for every season.

HOW DOES IT MAKE MONEY?

PKTS is the perfect direct to consumer brand. It has a simple and clear message and the target audience is likely tween girls or young women, two groups that spend a lot of time online and enjoy discovering new fashion brands. Side note: if you've spent any time on Netflix recently, you know that "tween culture" has never been more popular. These young ladies are fashionable, digitally connected, and seem to have easy access to their father's credit cards.

Plus, PKTS is the perfect brand for Instagram. What a fun forum to showcase the functionality and fashion of PKTS' pockets! What do you carry in *your* PKTS' attire?

WHAT'S THE CATCH?

The key to this business is selling clothing that doesn't typically come with pockets. However, that inevitably makes it difficult to expand into apparel that does. For example, it would be difficult for PKTS to sell jeans, leather jackets, or accessories. This company would depend entirely on driving enough sales from its core line of products.

Also, women's fashion trends sweep in and out faster than the Santa Ana winds. If the pocket-loving craze comes to an abrupt halt, so do the business prospects of this idea.

WHAT'S THE LIKELIHOOD OF SUCCESS?

Success Rating: 84%

While the idea of launching a women's clothing company is daunting (many self-proclaimed fashionistas have tried and failed), the success of PKTS lies within the simplicity of its message. I have no doubt that PKTS could be a modern, fresh, and fashion forward direct-to-consumer brand.

The After Party

Contributor: Teresa Day

WHAT IS IT?

Disclaimer: we're about to start talking about dead people. Like that kid in *The Sixth Sense*, but far less creepy. For those keeping track, that's the second Haley Joel Osment reference in this book (see: Secret Sender). Not going to lie – I didn't see that coming when I set out to write this.

The harsh reality is that we all die. But the meaning and implication of death varies widely among different people. For many, there's a strong spiritual or religious connection. For others, it simply reflects the end of life and the beginning of decomposition (I warned you, didn't I?). These different beliefs impact the difficult choices that people must make *before* they die about what happens to them *after* they die. Do I want a burial plot? Do I want my body cremated and ashes spread? Do I want to donate my body to science? All these options appeal to different people for different reasons, but there's a common thread among them: they're all quite depressing. Why does death, one of life's few certainties, have to be so darn sad all the time? Don't get me wrong, death *is* depressing. But does it have to be depressing into perpetuity? Cemeteries are gloomy places. Sure, there are some beautiful ones, but in general, people at cemeteries are sad because they were never intended to be places of joy. But what if you could change that? There are a lot of people who, when they die, don't want the party to end. It's time they had a burial option that reflects that desire.

Introducing The After Party, cemeteries for those who wish to be celebrated, not mourned, in the afterlife. Imagine a cemetery with bright colors, live music, and seasonal cocktails. A place where people go to have fun, not reflect in silence. The After Party has karaoke night, movie screenings, and one heck of an annual Halloween party. Why mourn someone staring quietly at a generic gray headstone while you could celebrate their memory by belting out the chorus to "Fear the Reaper," irony be damned? Look, The After Party isn't *for* everyone. Fortunately for us, the potential user base *is* everyone. For those who prefer the old-fashioned way, there are plenty of existing burial plots for you to choose from. But for those that never want the party to end, this is something you just might be interested in.

WHY IS IT NEEDED?

As the world evolves, so too do its traditions. Throughout history, death has been recognized and celebrated in a variety of ways. As younger generations become more pragmatic and less spiritual, it is only logical that evolution will continue. There are millions of people who want an opportunity for their life to be remembered in ways currently not available. The After Party could serve a niche market, but one that is currently being underserved.

HOW DOES IT MAKE MONEY?

Not only does The After Party make money the usual way (people pay money for burial plots), but it also has a series of incremental revenue streams. At a traditional cemetery, guests do not spend any money while visiting. Thus, the cemetery must charge high burial plot fees since this is the primary source of revenue. But, The After Party can offer lower burial plot costs because it also generates revenue through all the activities and concessions it offers throughout the year. The After Party is equal parts graveyard and events business.

WHAT'S THE CATCH?

I think this idea will resonate most strongly with young people, many of whom don't share the same traditional values as older generations. But therein lies the problem – young people aren't going to die for a while! This business idea might be like opening a whiskey distillery – there's a bit of a waiting period before you can truly launch.

WHAT'S THE LIKELIHOOD OF SUCCESS?

Success Rating: 66.6%

C'mon, *The Sixth Sense... Fear the Reaper...* I'm essentially only an Al Pacino in *The Devil's Advocate* reference away from really driving this theme into the ground (or underground, in this case).

Printer Confidential

Contributors: Jeff Day & Kyle Banahan

WHAT IS IT?

Anyone who has worked in a corporate office environment knows that the best secrets aren't revealed behind closed office doors, but rather in an area accessible to everyone: the printer room. That's right. Many a tale, both professional and personal, could be told from items mistakenly left at the office printer. I think Xerox should change its slogan to "Oh, the stories I could tell." In fact, the sequence of events that occurs when you discover something at the printer that you weren't meant to see goes something like this:

Step 1: Immediately turn head toward the exit door to see if anyone is coming;

Step 2: Quickly shuffle through the pages you're not supposed to be looking at by pretending that your own print-outs may have somehow found their way into the middle of them;

Step 3: Immediately tell your best friend at work what you've discovered. Because, as we all know, a secret is only a secret if you tell someone.

Currently, entertaining printer stories are limited to where you work or those shared by close friends, but what if there was a way to relish in everyone's "found this at the office printer" tales of discovery?

Introducing Printer Confidential, an entertainment website and social media account that shares user-generated images of embarrassing, funny, and/or scandalous print-outs accidentally left at the company printer. There's a social media account for pretty much everything these days. Printer Confidential can become a must-follow account for bite-sized daily entertainment.

WHY IS IT NEEDED?

People literally can't get enough daily entertainment from social media. People spend over two hours a day on their phones shuffling through content at the speed of a thumb swipe. Entertainment accounts have millions of followers and source all their content from users. Remember the good old days when people would bring newspapers into the bathroom stall? Goodbye Wall Street Journal; Hello Instagram. There's no

denying the market demand for entertaining bite-sized daily content. The difficult part is finding a niche that hasn't already been taken. And for what it's worth, Dunder Mifflin already proved that paper isn't as boring as it may seem.

HOW DOES IT MAKE MONEY?

Like all social media businesses, Printer Confidential makes money in a way that truly perplexes anyone over the age of 65. Acquire followers; convince brands your followers are worth engaging with; sell advertising revenue. Printer Confidential will appeal to white-collar young professionals, a cohort that is attractive to businesses because they have disposable income and love to spend it frivolously.

WHAT'S THE CATCH?

The law. Yep, I think you may want to consult a lawyer before launching this one. Is the corporate office a legally protected area? Might you get fired for sharing someone's secrets? Don't ask me. These are half-baked, remember?

WHAT'S THE LIKELIHOOD OF SUCCESS?

Success Rating: 28%

Printer Confidential has some potential. It's easy to start, requires virtually no capital, and sources all its content from users. But a business like this requires momentum. Users will only interact with the platform if the content is entertaining. Acquiring initial users (and content) won't be immediate and will require some patience. That said, there's no reason Printer Confidential couldn't acquire millions of followers. And with millions of followers comes the potential for millions of dollars.

Sleeping with Friends

Contributor: Reverend Love

WHAT IS IT?

There's not much better than crawling into a freshly made bed with clean sheets. Yet, for most of us, we don't wash our sheets nearly as often as we're supposed to. Why? Because it's a pain or we're just too lazy (see: college students). What if there was a way to get the benefit of fresh sheets without the hassle of actually washing them?

Introducing Sleeping with Friends, a subscription bed linens service that delivers clean sheets directly to your home. Users select the type of sheets they want and how often they are delivered, both of which can be modified at any time. This allows users to experience sleeping on different types and quality of sheets. Most importantly, it means you never have to wash your own sheets ever again. When fresh sheets arrive, you simply toss the used sheets in a pre-paid return box, and voila, they're out of your life forever (or at least until they are cleaned and returned to you).

WHY IS IT NEEDED?

Of course, while not everyone needs this special service, several groups of people might benefit greatly from Sleeping with Friends:

First, busy moms. As any mom with a few kids will tell you, she spends more time doing laundry than practically anything else. Kids are filthy little creatures whose bed hygiene is borderline criminal. Moms and Dads would croon over a service like this one.

Second, lazy college students. Need I say more? Back in the day, I was lucky to wash my sheets once a semester. While the state of my sheets didn't necessarily bother me, it did disappoint one very important person – my mother. That demographic will gladly pay for this service to have one less thing to worry about while their kids are off at college.

Last, urban dwellers. If you've spent any time living in a densely populated city, you know that the chances of having a washer/dryer in your unit are about as good as having a closet that accommodates all your clothes (See: Seasons Change). It's tough enough walking seven blocks to get your undergarments washed, not to mention your sheets. This is for all the "do you have four quarters for a dollar" city folk.

HOW DOES IT MAKE MONEY?

Sleeping with Friends operates like a traditional paid subscription service. Users can customize various combinations of clean sheet frequency and linen quality - at different price points. The company can generate additional revenue with exclusive partnerships and promotions paid for by linens manufacturers. In fact, Sleeping with Friends can also act as a direct-to-consumer retailer and sell sheets to customers who no longer wish to rent. It's like trying on a pair of shoes before you buy them. But in this case, those shoes are 1,200 thread count Egyptian Cotton.

WHAT'S THE CATCH?

There are two clear roadblocks to success. First, while this service solves the problem of sleeping on clean sheets, it doesn't solve the frustration of having to actually make the bed. Second, you have to "share" sheets with strangers (hence the name of the business). The sheets are professionally laundered between uses, but for many, sharing sheets is something they reluctantly accept at hotels, not in their own homes.

WHAT'S THE LIKELIHOOD OF SUCCESS?

Success Rating: 33%

Sleeping with Friends addresses a common frustration, but might be hindered not only because of service cost, but emotional cost as well. Unless you want to sleep with thousands of strangers. Or as we like to call them, friends.

Suns Out Buns Out

Contributor: Teresa Day

WHAT IS IT?

Unless you've been living under a rock, you must have taken notice of the men's hairstyle trend sweeping the nation: the Man Bun. That's right. The Faux Hawk, Southern Swoop, and Hipster Fade have all had their chances to shine, but the man bun is having its moment in the sun. Despite having such beautiful hair to put on display, having a Man Bun doesn't mean that you've lost interest in occasionally wearing a ball cap. But what if you wanted to wear a cap while also showing off the Man Bun you worked so hard for?

Introducing Suns Out Buns Out (SOBO), a ball cap designed for hair in buns. SOBO simply modified the placement of the hole to accommodate the head location of the bun. Ball caps have stayed largely the same for years despite evolving hairstyles. It's time you designed a cap to meet the needs of hair rather than the other way around. And SOBO is not just for guys. Ladies can enjoy SOBO as well! Remember that scene in Apollo 13 where the NASA scientist told his engineers they need to find a way to fit a square peg into a round hole? Well, you're the scientist, baby! You did it! And c'mon, SOBO is sure to change the world more than any little moon landing. So, when the sun's out and you need a hat, don't get caught without your bun.

WHY IS IT NEEDED?

Do you wear Von Dutch trucker hats? Have you ever sported a turtle-neck? What about ripped acid washed jeans? This is fashion. SOBO is fashion.

Look, SOBO isn't *really* needed. I haven't heard a lot of men (or women for that matter) demanding a solution for this problem (or lack thereof). But this is a fashion statement. And when it comes to fashion, "need" is a four-letter word. But so what if SOBO isn't really needed. Neither were trucker hats. SOBO could work because it is unique and fun. And when it comes to how you look, this can be very appealing, even if short-lived. Just ask anyone who ever got a lower back tattoo.

HOW DOES IT MAKE MONEY?

Pretty simple. People buy hats. This business can be built online with sales direct to the consumer. SOBO requires a strong social media campaign and content that is worthy of sharing. Is it a long-term viable business? Maybe not. But could you capitalize on a trend to make a million bucks? Absolutely.

WHAT'S THE CATCH?

Fashion is fickle and hard to predict. Consumers might get a kick out of the idea but fail to purchase. It's impossible to predict the next Snuggie.

WHAT'S THE LIKELIHOOD OF SUCCESS?

Success Rating: 48%

Suns Out Buns Out is a novelty play. It requires timely entry, a success-ful digital marketing campaign, and good timing on the exit side. Or a celebrity endorsement from Leonardo DiCaprio who seems to like ugly hats (not a strategy to depend on). But with a creative social campaign and a few lucky bounces, could you sell 30,000 SOBO hats and generate a million dollars in sales? Absolutely.

Red Pill Adventures

Contributor: Mike Henry

WHAT IS IT?

Stop for a minute and think about all the membership clubs that exist. There are country club and gym memberships. There are book clubs and wine of the month memberships. There are fraternal societies and motorcycle clubs. There are now even restaurant and bar memberships (shout out Soho House). Heck, you can even be a club member at Costco! The point is that people *love* belonging to a club. They allow you to meet like-minded people and give you access to things you presumably enjoy. For some that's golf. For others it's a vintage cabernet. But most of these clubs are quite narrow in scope and require a depth of interest in the topic to justify the cost of membership. But what about the gluttony of young people with disposable income that crave the opportunity to participate in a variety of unique experiences, not just one activity? It's time for a club that doesn't provide access to things, but rather experiences.

Introducing Red Pill Adventures, a membership club that guarantees access to unique experiences. This club isn't about shared interest in one specific topic, but rather the collective appreciation for a diversity of experiences. Red Pill Adventures organizes exclusive events and experiences for its members, many of which may be impossible to participate in otherwise. Red Pill doesn't just plan a cooking class, but rather organizes a dinner hosted by a celebrity chef. Red Pill doesn't just tell its members to go see a concert, but rather hosts a private acoustic performance by Sheryl Crow. Because at Red Pill Adventures, every day really is a winding road. You get the point. Instead of members paying money to access a nice golf course, users pay money for experiences they can't easily get anywhere else and that are already organized for them.

WHY IS IT NEEDED?

People inherently want plans, they just don't necessarily want to be the one to make them. It takes a lot of time and energy to research, plan, and organize an activity. That's why there's often great pleasure in being told what to do. Everyone has that one friend who's really good at organizing events. But then that friend gets married, has kids, and starts taking their job seriously - leaving far less time for planning activities for the rest of us. Well, Red Pill Adventures is like having a hundred of those friends (the version without kids and a career, of course).

For many people, the scariest question they're asked at work has nothing to do with their job. It's "what are you doing this weekend?" Buying membership into Red Pill Adventures is like having a trump card to throw anytime that question is asked. "Oh, I'm just skydiving with the 101st Airborne on Saturday." * Mic drops. * Young people with disposable income and excess time are looking for ways to spend it, especially if it gives them bragging rights. It's hard to go into a store and buy a unique experience, which is why people will be waiting in line to pay for membership into Red Pill Adventures.

HOW DOES IT MAKE MONEY?

Red Pill Adventures is a national organization that operates individual chapters in select cities. Users pay a monthly membership fee to belong to the club. This grants them access to regularly planned unique experiences. Members then also pay to participate in each activity.

WHAT'S THE CATCH?

Users' willingness to pay for membership hinges on two things: First, the quality and uniqueness of the experiences. Second, the appeal of the members themselves. Like any club, you only want to join if the other members are people you want to socialize with. That's why Red Pill Adventures is by invitation only. New members are only admitted through the endorsement of existing members, not unlike a fraternity. It's how you'll prevent Red Pill Adventures from being the social outlet for nerds nationwide, otherwise known as Magic: The Gathering.

WHAT'S THE LIKELIHOOD OF SUCCESS?

Success Rating: 76%

Red Pill Adventures is one of those business ideas that I wish already existed so that I could join it. I have disposable income that I'm willing to spend on unique experiences that are already planned for me. Like Neo, I want to see where the red pill takes me.

Tipster

Contributor: Joey Davis

WHAT IS IT?

Look inside your wallet or purse and see how many one-dollar bills you have right now. For most of you, the answer will be none. That's because people don't carry a lot of cash on them anymore. Nowadays, people exchange money almost exclusively electronically. You can swipe a plastic card, swap money through texts, or pay in cryptocurrency (whatever the #$@! that is). Despite the prevalence of digital payment, there's still one thing we do that requires cold, hard cash: ~~marijuana~~ tipping. And I'm not talking about the kind of tip you add to a restaurant bill. I'm referring to all of the services where it's customary to throw a couple of bucks to someone who helped you out. Whether they parked your car, cleaned your golf clubs, or danced on your lap. Herein lies the problem, we often feel the need to tip a buck or two, but don't have the cash on hand required to do so.

Introducing Tipster, a pocket-sized device that holds and dispenses bills one at a time with the click of a button. It holds approximately 50 one-dollar bills, or whatever denomination you want. You stuff it with cash, and your tips will last. Tipster isn't meant to replace your wallet as an everyday item in your pocket. Instead, Tipster is available when and where you need it. Going on vacation? Throw Tipster in your suitcase. Heading to the country club? Keep a Tipster in your golf bag. No more sifting through your wallet looking for a dollar bill you know isn't there. With Tipster you'll never be called cheap behind your back ever again.

WHY IS IT NEEDED?

I'm not sure when or how it happened, but somewhere along the line, we started tipping for everything. As if paying $4 for a coffee wasn't enough already. While you can add a gratuity to most purchases, the same cannot be said for many services. It's not as if the hotel bellhop is carrying around a Square for you to swipe your credit card (and let's hope it never comes to that). For the indefinite future, there will remain a need to have easy access to small increments of cash.

HOW DOES IT MAKE MONEY?

Look, Tipster is a simple "make it cheaply overseas and sell it for a decent profit in the U.S. business model." Nothing new here. What is novel, however, is the direct sales method it could employ. Tipster will hire an army of commission-based sales reps. Who's in this army, you ask? It's filled with valet drivers, hotel bellhops, coat check attendants, country club bag boys, and the guys who dry your car at the carwash. Every time they lose out on a tip because the person didn't have any cash or small bills, they're presented with a perfect opportunity to sell the Tipster. In the embarrassment of the moment for the non-tipper, closing the sale will be easy. A Tipster is sold, the sales rep makes a commission, and the non-tipper feels a little less cheap. Everybody wins.

WHAT'S THE CATCH?

Tipster holds and dispenses cash, but it doesn't get the cash for you. It's hard enough to come by any cash these days, nevertheless one-dollar bills. Filling up your Tipster will most likely require a trip to the bank (unless of course you're one of those people that gets paid in tips). Going to the bank may not seem like a big deal to anyone over the age of 50, but for millennials, walking into a bank is as foreign of a financial concept as balancing a checkbook. People want cash, but do they want it bad enough to make a trip to the *bank*? I'm not so sure.

WHAT'S THE LIKELIHOOD OF SUCCESS?

Success Rating: 28%

Tipster might be one of those items that is purchased but never used. A stocking stuffer from Mom that ends up in the back of a sock drawer. While that means it might not have an enduring legacy, that doesn't prevent it from making a quick buck. Or two.

InSky InSights

Contributor: Jeff Day

WHAT IS IT?

Consumer research is a massive industry. Companies want to know what consumers think and are willing to pay big to find out. Today, companies will often hire a market research company to field online surveys. The research company has a database of consumers they've spent years collecting and to whom they pay a fee for completing a survey. These respondents (and let's face it, they're generally the type of people who are willing to do jury duty) are compensated for their time to log onto their computer and answer a series of questions. But, what if we could dramatically reduce the cost of completing a survey not by looking inward, but rather by looking up?

Introducing, InSky InSights, a consumer market research platform that uses airline passengers as a sample group to answer questions for clients. InSky InSights takes advantage of a basic human emotion: boredom. Like prisoners (who are unfortunately a difficult group to profit from), airline passengers are both bored and confined. SkyMall Magazine took advantage of this phenomenon for years before recently going out of business (RIP). My god, where else could you get otherwise rationale people to purchase a cat relaxation pod or zombie yard decorations? InSky InSights offers passengers the opportunity to answer digital survey questions for compensation. That compensation could be anything from a free cocktail to airline reward miles to actual money. But, the underlying principle is that these passengers would require far less compensation than a typical survey respondent.

As you're reading this half-baked idea, there are 700,000 people in the air *right now*. These passengers are diverse, strapped down to a chair, and convincing themselves that the unforgivably awful movie Downsizing might still be worth watching (c'mon Matt Damon). Let's give these passengers an alternative, one that we just so happen to profit from.

WHY IS IT NEEDED?

There are two things that drive companies crazy when it comes to consumer market research: it is expensive and takes too much time. InSky InSights solves both problems. The platform can dramatically lower costs (for reasons already described) and reduce time (since the large sample size of respondents allows surveys to be completed faster). Plus, consumer satisfaction with airlines isn't particularly great these days (cue video of United passenger dragged off a plane) so a service that rewards passengers would presumably be looked upon favorably.

HOW DOES IT MAKE MONEY?

This business model could work in a variety of ways (this is only half-baked, remember?). But for simplicity, let's assume that market research companies pay InSky InSights a small fee per completed survey. In turn, InSky InSights compensates both the airline (for giving it distribution) as well as the passenger (for completing the survey). You'll let much smarter people figure out the rest.

WHAT'S THE CATCH?

This feels overwhelmingly complicated to pull off. Unlike some of the ideas in this book, InSky InSights requires legitimate software technology and partnership with a complicated and heavily regulated industry.

WHAT'S THE LIKELIHOOD OF SUCCESS?

Success Rating: 19%

I like this idea, probably because I used to work for a consumer research company and travel frequently. But, cracking into a billion-dollar industry filled with government regulation? Not sure I am quitting my day job to start this one.

One and Done

Contributor: Reverend Love

WHAT IS IT?

In a somewhat ironic way, going to the bathroom sort of reminds me of having to fill your car up with gas. Sure, the fluids are traveling in different directions, but they share several of the same principles. It's something you must do every few hours while in use, there are designated areas to do it, and there is often a waiting line. Most of the time these rules don't bother us, but there are certain occasions where we'd do almost anything for a better solution. For hundreds of years, men have found that solution in the form of woods, empty beer bottles, and even adult diapers. Those methods are not only rudimentary, but also limited in their applicability. We may not be quite ready to fill up our cars outside of gas stations, but the time for a urination revolution is now.

Introducing One and Done, men's briefs and boxers that allow you to pee directly into a leak-proof disposable bag without ever getting up. While the idea is crass, the design is nothing short of sophisticated. There is a slim plastic O-ring on the overlap of the fly which connects to medical-grade ½ liter plastic bags. The bag is slim profile, so it sits down the pant leg and has a curved top to avoid blockage. You simply attach a bag discretely under your shorts, slip your johnson through the "O" and commence peeing. Once fully relieved, remove the bag and close with our leak-proof seal and toss into the nearest available garbage. Naturally, of course, One and Done uses biohazard quality bags so they are safe to throw in public trash. This idea is pure gold (pun intended).

WHY IS IT NEEDED?

One and Done is a product for men who are in an environment not conducive for pee breaks. Whether you're working a construction site, attending a sporting event, or just a trucker on a long road trip, you don't want to be inconvenienced by the traditional necessities of emptying the tank. When a football game resumes play in the third quarter, you want to know why the stadium only looks half filled? Because everyone is still in line at the bathroom. Many a brilliant play has been missed by waiting for a vacant urinal outside section 112. With One and Done, you'll never miss a play again.

Heck, One and Done might even be popular among men in college fraternities. Not because they don't have access to bathrooms, but because they're, well, frat guys.

HOW DOES IT MAKE MONEY?

One and Done works like the razor blade model. In this case, the boxers are the razor and the bags are the blades. Users only need to purchase the boxers once, but with every successful urination, another bag is sold. You go one, you sell one, if you will.

In addition to selling our own boxers, there are also licensing opportunities with the O-ring. I can already see it now, a commercial for "Fruit of the Loop with Go Anywhere technology."

Lastly, let's not forget about brand expansion. Why stop at One and Done when you could launch Two and Through?

WHAT'S THE CATCH?

Remember that scene in *Dumb and Dumber* where Jim Carrey is relieving himself in empty beer bottles while driving? You may recall that the biggest problem wasn't the act of peeing in the bottle itself, but rather the moment in which he recognized that one bottle wasn't enough. Will One and Done suffer the same fate?

Surely there are several other health and safety related issues with this concept that I will whiz by for now.

WHAT'S THE LIKELIHOOD OF SUCCESS?

Success Rating: 61%

One and Done is at the intersection of three concentric circles of a Venn diagram. Those circles are represented by the male gender's Affinity for Drinking, Laziness, and General Disregard for Human Decency. The intersecting portions of those circles have been big enough to accommodate inventions like the drinking helmet. Why should this be any different?

Listed

Contributor: Lars Weborg

WHAT IS IT?

Really the only thing worse than moving is having to tell everyone you moved. And for many people between 22-35 years old, this is something that happens every 1-2 years. It typically necessitates a mass email with the subject heading "We've Moved!" or some quirky over-thought variation of such. And even though it is you who moved, your friends and family are required to spend effort updating their records with your new mailing address, a place in which you're almost sure to depart prior to them ever sending you anything. This feels broken, right? The rest of us shouldn't have to exert any energy updating contact information for people who move. The onus should be on the ones doing the moving.

Introducing Listed, a platform that shares up-to-date contact information with your network. The basic idea is simple – a service that *pushes out* your contact information to those that are following you. For example, if I moved from Buffalo to Chicago, I would update my contact information once and presto, anyone following me would have access to my new address. With notifications on, they'd even get a message letting them know. This works not just for your mailing address, but any contact information you wish to share like your phone number; or perhaps even a buzzer (shout out doctors and retro drug dealers). With Listed, you'll always have up-to-date contact information for those in your network. The "what's your address again?" text will be a thing of the past. And everyone will be thankful for it.

WHY IS IT NEEDED?

There's probably a specific reason this idea was contributed by Lars, who happens to be a close friend. I have asked Lars for his address no fewer than a dozen times. And I can promise you (and him), if I need it again, I'll have to ask for it. I haven't the slightest idea what it is, and I don't have a good system for storing and updating addresses. If, however, I was following Lars on Listed, this wouldn't be an issue. And perhaps he wouldn't scold me every time I ask. Listed: saves you time and friendships.

HOW DOES IT MAKE MONEY?

This is a tech company, right? Then who cares about how it makes money. You're only looking for a million-dollar idea. In Silicon Valley, they'd probably give you a million bucks just for showing them the napkin sketch. This business will follow the same model as every other over-valued tech startup: get a whole bunch of users and figure out how to make money later.

WHAT'S THE CATCH?

There's not a single idea that starts with "it's an app..." that hasn't already been thought of by some twenty-one-year-old in Silicon Valley. By the time this book is released, this product will probably already exist, if it doesn't already. And if not, it's probably because it failed to establish product-market fit (or whatever the tech nerds say these days). It is with good reason that this book contains very few "it's an app that..." ideas. We'll leave those to the kids still living in their parents' basements.

WHAT'S THE LIKELIHOOD OF SUCCESS?

Success Rating: 21%

This idea gets the same chance of success as the likely age of the person who creates it.

Laptop Bjorn

Contributor: Jeff Day

WHAT IS IT?

We live in an era of constant connectivity. Long gone are the days of leaving your computer at the office. In fact, employees are so connected that even as they're on-the-go, they feel compelled to be working. Just look at any corporate office. People aren't socializing as they walk from room to room; they're on their phones checking emails (or at least pretending to in order to avoid small talk with the creepy IT guy walking nearby). Checking your phone works well for certain things, but it pales in comparison to the functionality of your laptop. Yet it's awkward and clumsy to try and work on your laptop while on-the-go. If only you had free hands to enjoy the full functionality of your laptop while walking from place to place.

Introducing Laptop Bjorn, a wearable carrier for your laptop that allows you to work while walking. The Laptop Bjorn works just like a baby carrier, except instead of holding an adorable baby, it holds your not-so-cute laptop. This contraption allows you the freedom to work while walking. If you work in a large corporate office, it can be worn walking between meetings to increase productivity. Want to get some exercise during the day? No problem. Throw on your Laptop Bjorn and get in your 10,000 steps while cleaning out your inbox. The Laptop Bjorn takes corporate multi-tasking to a whole new level. Best of all, it won't spit up on you.

WHY IS IT NEEDED?

Companies are doing anything they can to increase the productivity of their employees. From catered lunches so they never have to leave the building to installing treadmills with laptop docks, so they can work while working out. At the same time, employees are doing everything they can to increase their daily output. The Laptop Bjorn provides an alternative to working at your desk that is far superior than what your iPhone can offer. Companies can now offer employees the opportunity to walk and work without sacrificing efficiency. Move over standing desks and treadmills. The Laptop Bjorn has arrived kicking and screaming.

HOW DOES IT MAKE MONEY?

While the Laptop Bjorn could be sold directly to consumers, the bigger opportunity is to sell directly to corporations, who would provide them to its workforce for free. Companies have deep pockets and are willing to try anything to enhance workplace culture and productivity. I can envision the Facebook embroidered Laptop Bjorn as we speak.

WHAT'S THE CATCH?

Look, I'll be the first to admit: this idea is kind of silly. But, you know what else I thought was pretty silly? Those briefcase on wheels people roll around the office. If employees can get over the embarrassment of wheeling around their work bag, who's to say they can't get comfortable with the idea of carrying around their laptop?

WHAT'S THE LIKELIHOOD OF SUCCESS?

Success Rating: 16%

The Laptop Bjorn is a sign of the times. It's also borderline brilliant or really, really stupid. This idea really underscores the 'half-baked' in half-baked ideas.

No Vacancy

Contributor: Mike Henry

WHAT IS IT?

Drive past any Blockbuster Video or Toys "R" Us and you'll get a first-hand glimpse of a rising trend: vacant commercial real estate. It's no secret that the rise of e-commerce, along with a thousand other things, has contributed to the demise of many brick and mortar retailers. With that comes not only the emotional toll of seeing our childhood memories fade to extinction, but also the very practical implication of now vacant real estate. Airbnb helped create a billion-dollar industry by capturing the value of vacant homes, so why can't savvy (and panicked) landowners capture value out of their TJ Maxx that's been sitting empty for eight months?

Introducing No Vacancy, a marketplace brokering micro-leases for temporarily unused real estate. Ever want to watch a movie in a boarded-up Regal Cinemas? Throw a slumber party in a JCPenney's? Or perhaps host your own version of "Supermarket Sweep" in a closed down grocery store? Now you can. Halloween stores have pioneered this model for short-term pop-up stores, but No Vacancy takes it to a whole new level.

WHY IS IT NEEDED?

No Vacancy helps connect two highly motivated groups of people: property owners who are looking to make money, and individuals who are looking to host a unique experience. It gives them access to space for pennies on the dollar. Vacant space could also be used for marketing purposes. Can you imagine if AMC had promoted an upcoming season of Breaking Bad by opening a pop-up Los Pollos Hermanos chicken restaurant in an unused Popeye's location? Or if HBO promoted Westworld by renting a country bar and turning it into the Mariposa Saloon? The possibilities are endless!

HOW DOES IT MAKE MONEY?

Like any middle man, you take a cut of the transaction.

WHAT'S THE CATCH?

Have you ever been inside an abandoned commercial property? Not everyone makes it past the meth heads and animal feces that greet you at the entrance. For this business to work, the vacant real estate must be kept clean and operational – otherwise no one would rent it. This of course costs money. Properties would need to be rented with enough frequency to justify keeping the lights on, if you will. Are there enough people or businesses out there who want to host a dance party in an empty Media Play? I'm not quite sure.

WHAT'S THE LIKELIHOOD OF SUCCESS?

Success Rating: 7%

Brokers depend on scale. When you take a small piece of the action, you need a lot of action. Unlike home rentals, No Vacancy attempts to solve what may not actually be a problem, but rather a fantasy. And unless you're Walt Disney or Hugh Hefner, it's not always easy to make money from fantasies.

Help, I've Fallen! Collections

Contributor: Leslie Day

WHAT IS IT?

We're all familiar with the "Help! I've Fallen and I Can't Get Up!" info-mercials, right? Life Alert is a medical alert system designed to protect seniors by providing emergency service with the push of a button (worn as a bracelet or necklace). It's an ingenious service and claims to have saved over half a million lives since 2008. The only problem is that it also appears their product offering hasn't changed since that time either. While the functionality of the service is undeniable, the aesthetics leave much to be desired. Seniors may not be known for their style, per se, but that doesn't mean they shouldn't look good. Function, it's time to meet fashion.

Introducing Help, I've Fallen! Collections, a jewelry line for seniors that beautifully integrates Life Alert help systems into necklaces, pendants, and bracelets. This jewelry line offers a variety of pieces that allow seniors to easily pop in and pop out their alert system button. Saving lives has never looked so good.

WHY IS IT NEEDED?

Because the current offering looks like it was designed by a middle school PE teacher. Wearing a rope necklace might work for Coach Rus-sel, but our elders deserve better. Just because they're old doesn't mean they've stopped trying to look good. Well, I guess some have. But still. Plus, can you imagine how much fun the Help, I've Fallen! Collections runway show would be? Talk about a viral marketing campaign.

HOW DOES IT MAKE MONEY?

The key to this business is a successful partnership with Life Alert, or one of the major players in this space. They benefit because the jewelry should make seniors more likely to buy and wear their hardware. The company benefits because anytime someone buys a Life Alert system, they'll be presented with the opportunity to buy a product. It's like buying a case for your phone.

WHAT'S THE CATCH?

There isn't one, hence why they fall...

Sorry, I couldn't resist.

In truth, the consumer wearing a Life Alert system probably isn't out doing a ton of shopping or swiping through their Instagram feed discovering new products. This is a tricky consumer to reach and it might require an old-school marketing approach (no pun intended). Additionally, companies are supposed to evaluate the cost of customer acquisition as well as the lifetime value of that customer. Well, let's be honest, the lifetime value of someone wearing this jewelry might be a bit short, if you know what I mean.

WHAT'S THE LIKELIHOOD OF SUCCESS?

Success Rating: 65%

A person over the age of 65 is defined as a "senior." In legislation, this term applies to the age at which pensions, social security, or medical benefits for the elderly become available. This milestone also feels quite appropriate for the success rating of Help, I've Fallen! Collections. Seniors are an underserved segment and this jewelry collection could be the first of its kind.

Mic'd Up

Contributor: Jeff Day

WHAT IS IT?

Americans love sports. Technology has enabled fans and viewers to feel closer to the games than ever before. And social media has enabled us to feel closer to the players. In recent years, game broadcasts have mic'd certain players and edited the footage into a family-friendly piece of content. It's better than nothing, but it makes us crave so much more. In fact, many fans would be willing to pay a premium for even greater access.

Introducing Mic'd Up, a pay-per-view sports network that offers uncensored audio of players and coaches throughout the game. This service is an incremental offering to existing sports programming. Mic'd Up is for fans that want to feel even closer to game action. And by action, I'm primarily referring to the trash talking. People can choose to watch a game on the regularly scheduled broadcast (as they've always done) or upgrade to watch it on Mic'd Up. For a fee, viewers will have unprecedented access to players and coaches, all of whom are mic'd up prior to, during, and after the game. Fans will be able to experience the game like never before. They'll be able to hear what linebackers actually say to quarterbacks after a sack, what basketball players say to celebrities sitting courtside, and what baseball players say to each other to pass the time during a baseball game.

Mic'd Up is a way to capitalize on fan's insatiable love for their teams and the personalities of the players.

WHY IS IT NEEDED?

Sports is in the entertainment business. We, the fans, wish to be entertained (cue Russell Crowe in *Gladiator*). As TV ratings continue to decline, Mic'd Up gives fans a new reason to come back. Heck, people wait all year for the chance to watch a four-episode season of HBO's *Hard Knocks*. Viewers can't get enough of the unprecedented access to players. It also doesn't hurt that the soundtrack is exceptional.

In fact, viewers have been paying to watch sports for years. Wrestling, Boxing, and UFC all have regularly scheduled pay-per-view events that make a fortune. Sports fans are a rabid bunch that will gladly pay for breadcrumbs.

HOW DOES IT MAKE MONEY?

At first, it might be too difficult to make every game available for Mic'd Up. The service can be tested by piloting the platform with marquee matchups and making them available for purchase. Viewers pay a fee to watch uncensored games which more than offsets the cost of production and broadcast rights. I don't know about you, but I would gladly pay $50 to hear what's being said at the bottom of a pile up.

WHAT'S THE CATCH?

The fans might want it, but the players and leagues surely won't. Players would hate the idea of being mic'd up for every game and the leagues would be (rightfully) concerned about the image it might portray. Plus, full access to player and coach audio would allow other teams to learn all the calls and signals of the opposing team, something the players union would certainly not be in favor of.

Aside from the inevitable pushback from the players and league, I can't begin to imagine the technical challenges of pulling this off and the cost and complexity of broadcast rights. This idea is better left to the pros.

WHAT'S THE LIKELIHOOD OF SUCCESS?

Success Rating: 2%

The likelihood of Mic'd Up becoming a reality is like that of the Cleveland Browns winning a Superbowl. Most people are rooting for it, but it's unlikely to ever happen (sorry, Cleveland. Again).

Hang Me Out to Dry

Contributor: Erin P.

WHAT IS IT?

Recently there's been a rise in direct to consumer do-it-yourself medical tests. Whether it's to assess your sensitivity to foods or to learn more about your ancestry, advances in technology have enabled users to feel comfortable self-administering tests that previously required experts and a doctor's visit to complete. The good news is that people are increasingly getting used to drawing their own blood. The bad news is that Maury Povich no longer has a monopoly on "who's the father" tests. The unfortunate news is, that despite many of these do-it-yourself advancements, there is not yet a solution that addresses the biggest problem of all: ~~early onset baldness~~ hangovers. That's about to change.

Introducing Hang Me Out to Dry, an at-home kit for self-administering an IV fluid drip. Move over Gatorade and McDonald's hashbrowns. Look, we all know that firefighters and medical students already do this anyway. This isn't reinventing the wheel, it's just making it easier to drive on. Hang Me Out to Dry uses a device that goes around the arm and automatically connects to the vein without the help of a trained professional. The technology hasn't been invented yet, but that's why this is only half-baked. Users then sit back, relax, and dry out. Until the next morning.

WHY IS IT NEEDED?

Because being hungover sucks. And despite there being a foolproof solution to avoid it (stop drinking), people refuse to acknowledge that as an option. In fact, professional services already exist that administer IV fluids, but they are expensive and need to be scheduled ahead of time. Customers need an on-demand solution, not one that needs to be scheduled 48 hours in advance and requires you to put on pants. Plus, the best (worst) hangovers are those that are unexpected.

While this business will initially focus on being a good hangover remedy, it can expand into drips for all sorts of ailments. Suffering from thirst? No problem, it'll hang you out to... hydrate.

HOW DOES IT MAKE MONEY?

The business model for Hang Me Out to Dry is similar to that of a Keurig coffee machine. A customer pays for the primary device (in this case, the easy-to-use device that hooks up to your arm) as well as individually-sold bags of fluid. Like Keurig, you'll break-even (or potentially even lose money) on the device itself but profit greatly from the sale of bags.

WHAT'S THE CATCH?

Well, sticking a needle directly into your vein isn't something most people have proficiency or interest in doing (turning a blind eye to the heroin epidemic sweeping the nation). So, this idea requires finding an alternative method to administering an IV bag. What's that method, you ask? Well, I'm no doctor, but you should be able to develop a tool that inserts a needle into your vein without the need of a trained medical professional. Plus, wouldn't we all trust a machine to do a better job at this anyway? I'm not saying I don't trust nurses, but why does it always seem that the nurse sticking a needle into your arm is doing it for the first time?

WHAT'S THE LIKELIHOOD OF SUCCESS?

Success Rating: 42%

Demand isn't the problem for this idea. Neither is price. All that stands between you and a million dollars is some medical technology and a whole bunch of malpractice attorneys.

Buuber

Contributor: Pete C.

WHAT IS IT?

Let's talk boobs. Not the ones your significant others catch you staring at, but rather those that perform one of nature's most important roles: breastfeeding. Moms all around the globe are supporting the growth of their newborns by working hard to produce nutrient rich milk. That milk needs to go *somewhere* to avoid clogs (we'll spare everyone the details). As such, breastfeeding moms will either "pump and store" or "pump and dump" excess milk. Storing the milk requires both a pump and a mechanism for traveling and keeping the milk cold or frozen. Dumping, on the other hand, requires the same equipment but the milk is ultimately wasted. Despite some of these challenges, more and more women are opting to breastfeed because of the important nutritional benefits it provides. Sadly, many moms can't breastfeed for a variety of reasons, and it's frustrating when your original feeding plan doesn't go your way – especially on top of the emotional toll of being a new mom. What if you could help the growing population of working moms who travel for work and those moms who, for whatever reason, can't breastfeed their own children?

Introducing Buuber, a service that connects breastfeeding moms away from their children with infants that need breast milk but can't get it. Instead of storing or dumping, this would allow moms to "pump and share." How would it work exactly? I'm not entirely sure (reminder: these are half-baked for a reason). But, thanks to Beyoncé we know that girls run the world, so I'm confident they'll figure it out.

WHY IS IT NEEDED?

When you read anything about parenting, one of the first things you'll learn is the important nutritional benefits of breastfeeding. It is so important to disease prevention that many insurance companies will incentivize both individuals and companies to participate. There's a reason your office has a "pump room." Insurance providers know that the benefit of building your child's immune system early on will save them money down the road. Despite knowing these benefits, many moms can't do it. At the same time, we've got moms with excess milk practically squirting out of their nipples. Buuber connects hungry kids with bursting moms. Forget about farm to table, this is boob to baby.

HOW DOES IT MAKE MONEY?

Throughout time perhaps nothing has been discussed more than how to profit off women's breasts. And while many of those businesses required the involvement of men, this one is decidedly female. Woman to woman. Mom to mom. Did I successfully avoid the question?

WHAT'S THE CATCH?

Did I mention that a mother would have to be comfortable allowing her child to drink another woman's breast milk? And that the breastfeeding mom would also have to be comfortable giving her milk to a stranger's child or even letting someone else's baby latch on to her? I know we're willing to share cars and houses with complete strangers, but I'm not sure we're quite ready for the breast sharing movement to begin.

WHAT'S THE LIKELIHOOD OF SUCCESS?

Success Rating: 11%

Buuber might have a great logo (you can picture it, right?) and be fun to say, but it feels operationally complex and emotionally charged.

Bobby's Buns

Contributor: Jeff Day

WHAT IS IT?

Remember that scene in *Father of the Bride* where Steve Martin gets arrested for going ham (pun intended) in the grocery store because he can only buy hot dogs in packages of 8 and buns in packages of 12? It's a great scene but has nothing to do with this business idea. I was just thinking about it since this idea is related to hot dogs. Side note on *Father of the Bride*: I could have sworn the husband in the movie was played by a young Paul Rudd. Turns out it's some guy named George Newbern who just so happens to be a poor man's Paul Rudd. The more you know...

We all love hot dogs and hamburgers. They are as American as apple pie. But when was the last time you put a traditional Oscar Mayer hot dog in a regular hot dog run? It's an atrocity. There's excess bread all over the place. It looks like a cute kid trying on dad's suit jacket. The key to a good hot dog or burger lies not only in the meat itself, but also in the all-too-overlooked bread-to-meat ratio.

Introducing Bobby's Buns, a bread company that sells "scooped out" hamburger and hot dog buns to ensure the optimal bread-to-meat ratio. These buns have a delicious and supportive exterior without all the extraneous dough on the inside. Bobby's Buns are named after celebrity chef, Bobby Flay. Bobby became famous for cooking the perfect burger, and the "scoop out" is a tactic he employed with great success. With Bobby's Buns, the scooping is already done for you. The only thing more American than hot dogs is the never-ending pursuit to perfect them.

WHY IS IT NEEDED?

Steve Martin's character was upset about the ratio in pack sizes between hot dogs and buns, but he would be equally displeased about the bread-to-meat ratio. How can something so American cause so much anguish? Plus, everyone knows that carb-filled bread isn't exactly good for you. Bobby's Buns optimize the eating experience while also helping you stay healthier. Except for the fact you're still eating a hot dog.

HOW DOES IT MAKE MONEY?

Bobby's Buns is a traditional food product that would be sold in retailers nationwide. You sell buns and shoppers buy them. Simple. With less bread in your buns, your margins should be nice and fat.

WHAT'S THE CATCH?

I didn't seek Bobby Flay's permission to use his name, so you may need to change the brand to avoid a lawsuit. But besides that, there's no catch. Make Hotdogs Great Again.

WHAT'S THE LIKELIHOOD OF SUCCESS?

Success Rating: 82%

Bobby's Buns should already exist. I hope the folks over at Wonder Bread are reading this because I just gave you your next big idea.

DormBox

Contributor: Anonymous

WHAT IS IT?

At any given time, there are about 20 million students attending American colleges and universities. That's a lot of kids who are poor and lazy and a lot of parents who are probably worried about them (with good reason). College students love free stuff and parents want to rest easy knowing their children have the essentials required to survive freshman year. Well, what if there was an effortless way for parents to regularly give their college aged kids boxes of useful "free" stuff?

Introducing DormBox, a monthly subscription box service for parents to support their kids who are away at college. DormBox is meant to be paid for by parents but enjoyed by their children who are at school. Every month, the student receives a DormBox package in the mail. Inside are a variety of college essentials and fun surprises. DormBox curates all the items so the experience is completely turnkey and effortless for parents (excluding the effort it takes to fork over their credit card information). The key is to find items that students want but that parents feel good about providing. Essentials may include items like toiletries, snacks, fresh socks (for the boys), school supplies, air fresheners, and a carabiner-affixed Nalgene water bottle (those were the days). DormBox makes it easy and affordable for parents to care about their kids and for kids to appreciate getting stuff their parents already paid for. Ah, the joys of parenting.

WHY IS IT NEEDED?

DormBox is needed because college kids - especially boys - can barely take care of themselves. Parents have enough to worry about with sex, drugs, and fraternity hazing. DormBox assures their child at least has snacks to eat and toothpaste to brush with. Many parents already send care packages to their kids at school, but this can be time-consuming and expensive. DormBox gives parents the benefits of caring about their kids without the hassle. Now *that's* a parenting hack.

Here's the real kicker: what do parents love most? Feeling appreciated and loved by their children. That's why every DormBox comes with a pre-stamped thank you card that allows students to write a thank you note back to their parents. Parents have a hard-enough time getting their kids to call them, nevertheless send a handwritten note. Talk about a retention strategy. If DormBox enables kids to send mail to their parents, they'll never stop paying for them!

HOW DOES IT MAKE MONEY?

DormBox makes money because Mom and Dad pay for it. What little money college kids have will inevitably go toward beer and pizza. Thus, this is a gifting business. The person paying for the service is different than the person receiving it. This business will initially target parents who send their kids to private schools. Why? Because it usually means two things: 1) they care a lot about their children, and 2) they have plenty of disposable income.

Once DormBox gets big enough, it will also benefit from brands who want their items included in the box. This will enable DormBox to get items for free or perhaps even charge an insertion fee to brands that want to reach a college audience.

WHAT'S THE CATCH?

DormBox is relatively foolproof, but there are a couple of limiting factors. First, maybe parents don't love their kids as much as I think they do. My mother would certainly have signed up for this service, but perhaps she's the gift-giving anomaly. Second, this business has a narrow window of time, four years to be exact, that it can profit from a given student. Graduation day might be a celebratory event for students and their families, but for DormBox, it's a time of great sorrow.

WHAT'S THE LIKELIHOOD OF SUCCESS?

Success Rating: 90%

In school metrics, this idea is an A. While there are a lot of subscription box services that don't pan out, DormBox is one that should. At $20/month for 12 months, this business needs less than 5,000 subscribers to gross a million dollars in sales. You don't need an IVY league education to do that math.

THE LAZY ENTREPRENEUR

ACKNOWLEDGEMENTS

Thank you to Erin P, Leslie D, Ian T, Kyle B, Phil E, Greg R, Ryan L, Neil P, Chuck F, Jimmy M, Pete C, Chris L, Cindy G, Kevin H, Ryan E, Aaron H, Tyler B, Teresa D, Scott S, Bill N, Lars W, Michael H, Adrienne B, Logan L, Blake H, Mike H, Jackie C, Joey D, Scott M, John E, Evan S, Roger K, Luis N, Collin F, Spike W, Mike M, Katie T, Nick M, Greg L, Taylor B, Caroline P, and Kasey L. for sharing your half-baked ideas with me. Without you, this book would not have been possible. Or at least a lot shorter. Sorry if I missed anyone.

Thank you to Jacque V, Lauren S, Halee B, Chris L, Leslie D, Rich D, Ben R, Laura, R, Katie B, Jen C, Spike W, Alon G, Steph V, and Matt A. for your feedback and editing help. It's nice to have smart and generous friends.

Thank you to Erin Leeder for your brilliant illustration work. Each one puts a smile on my face.

Thank you to Joanie Cahill for the wonderful cover art and your appreciation for "Easter eggs."

Thank you to my parents, Leslie and Rich, for well, *everything*.

Thank you to my wife, Teresa, for being the better half of our whole.

Thank you to Ryan and Scott for unknowingly giving me the confidence to publish this book.

Thank you to Casey Neistat for reminding me that intent without action means nothing.

Thank you to Ben & Jerry's for giving us *your* version of something half baked. It's the only ice cream allowed in my freezer.

Thank you to Will Smith for being one of the greatest entertainers of our generation (this is my book so I get to thank whoever I want, right?).

Last, thank you to Domino's Pizza. Not for having anything to do with this book, but for making all our lives just a little bit better.

THE LAZY ENTREPRENEUR

ABOUT THE AUTHOR

Ironically, Jeff Day is an entrepreneur and not quite as lazy as the book title would suggest. He is an accomplished brand marketer who has worked for Nielsen, General Mills, and Amplify Snack Brands, acquired by The Hershey Company in 2018. He earned his BA from Bucknell University and MBA from Northwestern's Kellogg School of Management. Jeff lives in Austin, Texas with his wife, Teresa. Most notably, he is a dedicated fan of the Buffalo Bills and knows that chicken wings should only be eaten with blue cheese, never ranch.

To contact Jeff, email him at halfbakedmilliondollarideas@gmail.com.

16173306R00097

Made in the USA
Middletown, DE
22 November 2018